Design
Sourcebook

JEWELLERY

Design Sourcebook

JEWELLERY

DAVID WATKINS

NEW HOLLAND

CONTENTS

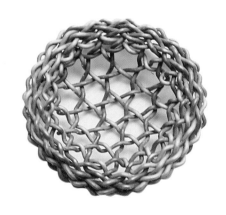

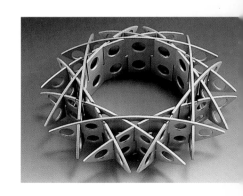

INTRODUCTION

THE OUTLOOK OF ARTIST JEWELLERS has developed immeasurably during the later years of the twentieth century. What was once the new territory of the isolated few has been colonized and opened up by the energy and enthusiasm of an army of newcomers – not only the makers, but also the collectors and devotees. The genre of contemporary jewellery is established and hitting its stride. It marches, however, in many directions.

Our survey takes in the work of over eighty jewellers from around the world. They are, of course, a small representation of the field, but their explorations encompass many forms, materials and concepts, stretching, challenging and sometimes revisiting traditional definitions in their search for expression. New themes break through as younger artists find their voices, and in general, formalism gives way to narration, intuition, the exploration of feeling, and the intersections of objects and relationships.

The commentary accompanying each artist jeweller discusses their work with reference to but also beyond the images chosen.

We resort to categories as devices to give clarity and intelligible order to

something that is inherently complex and evolving. The

distinctions are fluid. Although convergences may be seen and

sensed, they are no more than fleeting. No one artist fits neatly into a single

category. A closer view reveals an experimental interweaving, a borrowing and

overlaying of insights and sensibilities. This beautiful art, which focuses its gaze and its

practice so intimately on the individual spirit and senses of both maker and wearer, defies prescription.

Our book is dedicated to the emergent generation and to the next who will follow, inspired by them, for although the

mix is leavened by the accomplished creativity of some older, more established jewellers, its selection is weighted to the

developing vision and sincere commitment of those at earlier stages in their

explorations. They bear witness to the continuing vitality and potential of a

still new art form.

DAVID WATKINS

PROCESS, POETRY & MEANING

THIS CHAPTER CONTAINS TWO MAJOR THEMES, beginning in the main with artists for whom the generation of process and poetic meaning, through material and making, are inseparable elements of creation. It continues with artists for whom the communication of their own sensibilities and ideologies are paramount. The two interconnect, but not quite seamlessly.

Typically, phenomena of form and expression at first arise coincidentally or intuitively and are subsequently cultivated through observation and practice. This is a partnership in creativity – the maker must be alert.

"Little Sister as the Bride" - Necklace. Annelies Planteydt. 18ct gold, 24 ct gold. All parts connected and hammered on tension. 35 x 24 cm (14 x 9½ in). 1996

◬ **Treasures from Under the Sea (3). Tomomi Arata.** Silver, glass, enamel, sand. Cast in silver, set with glass stone, enamel and sand. Ø 17 mm (⅔ in). 1997

◬ **Treasures from Under the Sea (5). Tomomi Arata.** Silver, glass, enamel, sand. Cast in silver, set with glass stone, enamel and sand. Ø 17 mm (⅔ in). 1997

◑ **Treasures from Under the Sea (4). Tomomi Arata.** Silver, silver wire, glass, enamel, sand. Cast, set with glass stone, enamel and sand. Ø 16 mm (⅝ in). 1997

The jewellery of Tomomi Arata is quite unique and powerfully evocative.

In this series of rings, he has developed a process to replicate the encrustation and agglomeration, which signifies objects that have lain a long time on the ocean bed and have been absorbed into that fascinating subterranean world.

The process parallels the creative action of ocean and time but through the medium of the jeweller's skills. Heat, torch and flame, have fused silver, enamel, glass and sand into convincing metaphors. The result is absolutely poetic and utterly convincing. It is a strong concept and a real achievement to have interpreted natural phenomena in such a way.

◭ **Treasures from Under the Sea (1). Tomomi Arata.** Silver, glass, enamel, sand. Cast in silver, set with glass stone, enamel and sand. Ø 16 mm (⅝ in). 1997

◭ **Treasures from Under the Sea (2). Tomomi Arata.** Silver, glass, enamel, sand. Cast in silver, set with glass stone, enamel and sand. Ø 16 mm (⅝ in). 1997

 Ring (balloon deflated, see opposite). Sigurd Bronger.

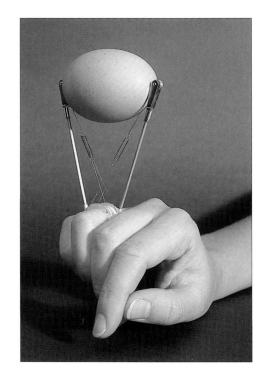

 White Egg-shaped Brooch. Sigurd Bronger. Eggshell, brass, steel. Fabricated, assembled. 16 x 5 cm (6¼ x 2 in). 1997

◐ **Ring. Sigurd
Bronger.** Eggshell, brass,
steel. Fabricated.16 x 5 cm
(2¼ x 2 in). 1997

△ **Ring. Sigurd
Bronger.** Valve, steel,
silver, balloon. Fabricated,
assembled. 7 x 2 cm
(2¾ x ¾ in); balloon
Ø 25 cm (10 in). 1997

*Sigurd Bronger introduces humour and a
strong sense of the surreal into jewellery
objects whose dominating aesthetic is
technical expression.*

*The delight with which Bronger exposes
the fashioning of miniature engineering
solutions to self-imposed "problems" is
palpable and infectious. This is jewellery
to make you smile – not only at the
humorous conceits it contains, but at the
enduring inventiveness and technical wit
of man.*

*This jewellery may not be primarily
wearable – it exists as much at the
crossing of engineering and art as it does
at the crossing of jewellery and sculpture
– but it serves well to illustrate a
fundamental, but rarely mentioned, truth
about the making of jewellery itself. Its
very scale – its miniature form – provides
the artist with an eminently manageable
test-bed for the pleasureable exercise of
skill and the playful exploration and
development of aesthetic themes and
motives.*

Brooch. Giovanni Corvaja. 18ct gold, 950 palladium, 22ct gold. Granulation. 7 x 7 cm (2¾ x 2¾ in). 1997

Giovanni Corvaja, from Padua, shows an outstanding command of the goldsmith's craft, placing him firmly in the great traditions of that city of goldsmiths.

The story of goldsmithing is one of respect for the accomplishments of those who have gone before and, equally, a determination to master them. According to its rules, success calls for knowledge, experimentation and finesse in the realms of technique, and originality in expression. Corvaja embraces this destiny. He has gained a great understanding of, and dexterity with, the coloured alloys of gold and the technique of granulation, and can turn these to truly poetic effect.

Photographs cannot really do justice to the painstaking research, the delicate fabrication of transparency or the subtle nuance of colour which account for his achievement.

Brooch. Giovanni Corvaja. 950 platinum, 22 ct gold. Granulation on platinum wires. Ø 7 cm (2¾ in). 1998

Brooch. Giovanni Corvaja. 22 ct gold and niello. Granulation. 6.5 x 6.5 cm (2½ x 2½ in). 1997

Rock Crystal. Lucy Sarneel.
Zinc, glass. Fabricated.
7 x 5 x 3.5 cm (2¾ x 2 x 1⅜ in).
1998

Forest Pond. Lucy Sarneel.
Zinc, perspex, gold. Fabricated.
5 x 4.5 x 2.5 cm (2 x 1¾ x 1 in).
1997

Lucy Sarneel's favoured material, zinc, assists in placing her jewellery in a metaphorical "no-man's land". The material itself has a dead greyness, yet her work shows unexpected signs of life in the suggestion of flower forms. There is a suspension between natural and unnatural – where everything seems still – also the hint that just as a piece of jewellery stands between the inner and outer life of the wearer, so it also draws life from this other exchange.

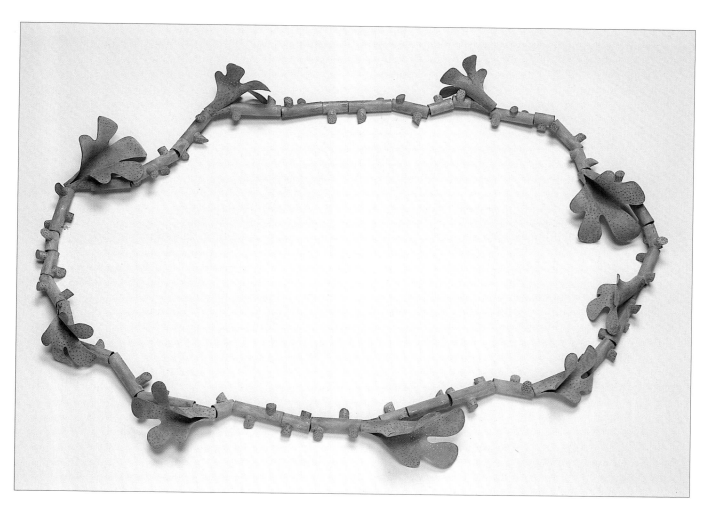

Koralijn. Lucy Sarneel.
Zinc, textile. Fabricated.
Ø neck opening 45 cm
(17¾ in). 1998

Sarneel's handling of the material is also evocative. Natural forms seem more remembered than observed, directly fabricated from raw metal, swiftly recorded in simple gestures, as if the span for such activity is precious and short, the moment critical. The result is a kind of testimony to the transitoriness of the vision – not negative, but affirmative.

Monika Brugger's shell-like silver brooches reflect her concern for the sympathy and respect which we should have for things in the world around us.

The metal, with its soft white surface, is worked until it is very thin and fragile, thus emphatically demanding careful handling. Its light weight means that a brooch can appear to alight on the garment with little disturbance. In

fact, the brooch is secured to the garment by the most minimal means – a hidden rubber ring which passes through the hole at the back. These pieces seem simply to fall from the sky, they are so delicate, insubstantial and mysterious.

▽ **Silence (back).**
Monika Brugger.

▽ **Silence (front).**
Monika Brugger. 950
silver. Fabricated.
Ø 9.2 cm (3⅝ in). 1998

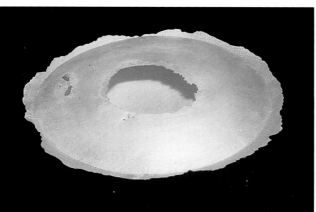

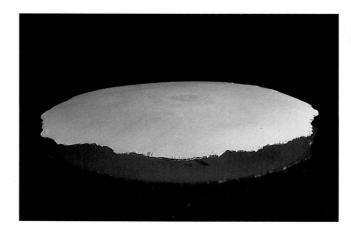

⬘ **Silence (back).**
Monika Brugger.

⬘ **Silence (front).**
Monika Brugger.
950 silver. Fabricated.
Ø 9.2 cm (3⅝ in). 1996

Necklace. Vered Kaminski. Stones, alpaka. Fabricated. Ø 20 cm (8 in). 1994

Vered Kaminski celebrates the gritty actuality of her urban environment, preferring poor and inconsequential materials to those of high investment value. In this series, the raw image of wire netting is combined with stone chips, their colour selected so that they refer to coral. Thus, just as the "coral" – representing nature – is trapped in its man-made lattices, the hard, unforgiving wire is also softened, compromised by such association, and yields to the imaginative insight of the maker.

The reference is to the impoverished but they are also powerful metaphors for life in uncertain circumstances, and invite us to consider that beauty must sometimes be where you find it – underfoot and in the streets.

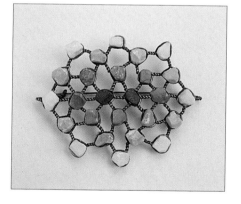

Brooch. Vered Kaminski. Stones, brass. Fabricated. 7.5 x 6 cm (3 x 2¼ in). 1991

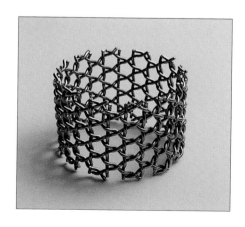

Bracelet. Vered Kaminski. Steel. Fabricated. Height 4.5 cm (1¾ in); Ø 7 cm (2¾ in). 1997

**Brooch "Sogno" (Dream).
Annamaria Zanella.** Iron, alpaka,
silver, gold, niello. Assemblage,
hammered iron and enamelled with
acid. 8 x 5 cm (3¼ x 2 in). 1996

*Annamaria Zanella is a "new" name
from Padua. In contrast to the Paduan
tradition of delicately-worked and refined
gold fabrication, she finds her
inspiration, and some of her material, in
the waste and dross of the industrial
landscape. This material she has in turn
"celebrated" as jewellery.*

*Starting from the point of "arte povera",
Zanella has explored aesthetic qualities
in the turnings or shavings of scrap from
machined steel, in corroded metal, broken
glass and so on, using them for their
own inherent expressiveness.*

*Now she has begun to use gold, often
surprisingly coloured, exploiting its
capacity to take on many complex
textures – some of them replicating or
suggesting the industrial detritus with
which she began – and to endure any
amount of working whilst maintaining
its own special integrity.*

 **Ring "Anello
Nuziale" (Wedding
Ring). Annamaria
Zanella.** Iron, glass,
pure gold.
Assemblage.
8 x 4.5 x 2.3 cm
(3¼ x 1¾ x ⅞ in).
1993

21

◆ **Brooch "Il Giorno e la
Notte" (Day and Night).
Annamaria Zanella.** Gold.
Hammered gold and
oxidation (blue) with acid.
7 x 4.5 x 3.2 cm
(2¾ x 1¾ x 1½ in). 1997

PROCESS, POETRY & MEANING

Vilhena is crucially interested in what he calls "the somewhat problematic distinction between jewellery as art and jewellery as objects for people".

22

▶ **Ring (from the installation 365). Manuel Vilhena.** Fine silver. Hand-wrought. Ø 2.2 cm (⅞ in). 1998

He explores the dynamic between jewellery as we see it – as an autonomous object – and the same jewellery when we have taken it and worn it – when it enters a new domain of relationship and definition. For this reason, he is emphatically concerned with aspects of presentation, combining individual pieces into gallery installations, which immediately objectifies them, before releasing them to users, which then also releases their other potential.

On the face of it, this amounts to a very simple and direct action – considering the complexities wrapped up in Vilhena's stated distinction – but of course it could not begin to work if his pieces were not also

beautifully crafted, seductive and subtly conceived examples of the jeweller's art in themselves. And, for all their simplicity, they are.

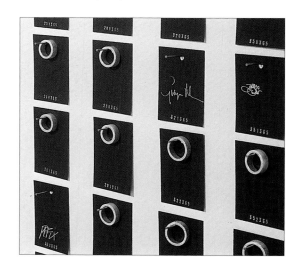

▲ **Three Hundred and Sixty-five (detail of installation). Manuel Vilhena.** Fine silver, cardboard, ink, iron nails. Hand-wrought, fusion welded (all rings have the same weight and were cut from a single 22 metre strip of material). 293 x 116 cm (115 x 45½ in) wide. 1998

Upside Down. Back to Front (series of four rings displayed upside down on glass stand). Manuel Vilhena. Blackened sterling silver, moonstones. Assembled. Each ring height 3.5 cm (1⅜ in), Ø 2 cm (¾ in); display height 14 cm (5½ in) 1998

The Missing Piece. Manuel Vilhena. 18 ct yellow gold box, glass ring. Box: assembled; ring: blown glass. (box contains two rings). 3.5 x 3.7 x 3.7 cm (1⅜ x 1⅖ x 1⅖ in). 1998.

Emi Fujita's cast glass jewellery falls into two distinct groups linked by an absolute love of the qualities of the material.

In the first group the pieces are truly wearable – rings or hand-sculptures. Here, glass is seen and represented as a living, fluid material – amorphous, slipping and sliding around the fingers – so that the hand and the glass become players in an erotic performance. In this performance, the weight and translucency of the glass is an important factor. The form of the glass is evidently sensual, but in effect the sensuality of the hand is thereby emphasized.

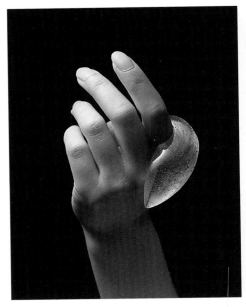

◯ **Glass Ring. Emi Fujita.** Glass. Kiln-worked. 3 x 6.5 x 5 cm (1¼ x 2½ x 2 in). 1998

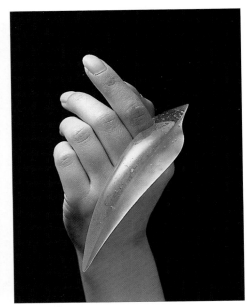

◯ **Glass Ring. Emi Fujita.** Glass. Kiln-worked. 3 x 13 x 4.5 cm (1¼ x 5¼ x 1¾ in). 1998

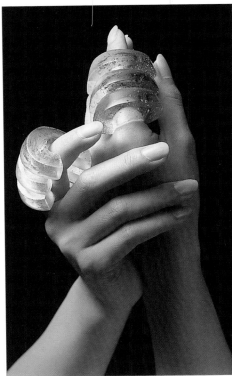

◯ **Glass Rings. Emi Fujita.** Glass. Kiln-worked. Rings on left: 2 x 4.5 x 4 5 cm (¾ x 2¾ x 2¾ in). 1998

**Glass Rings.
Emi Fujita.**
Glass, silver.
Kiln-worked and
lamp-worked
glass. Ring on
left:
11 x 4.5 x 2 cm
(4¼ x 1¾ x ¾ in).
1998

**Glass Rings.
Emi Fujita.**
Glass, silver.
Kiln-worked
glass. Ring on
far left:
9 x 9 x 1.5 cm
(3½ x 3½ x ⅝ in).
1998

The second group is quite different. In this case function is relinquished. The scale is uncertain, although the fact that it is miniature is important and contributes to its unreality. The ring – the subject of this exploration – has assumed a new identity. It has grown from the thing we wear to become a self-assured sculpture, referring to architecture and landscape. This work explores the spirit of the ring.

Andrea Wippermann tests the process of casting as a vehicle for expressive gesture.

This playful work to some extent revisits metaphors from sculpture in the immediate post-war years, its battered, mechanistic but anthropomorphic forms hint at personages and hierarchies. They are partway between figuration and abstraction with the complication of a need to introduce an element of communication within the pieces. One piece is tellingly entitled "Pair in Conversation".

Wippermann's vision is uncommon in present-day jewellery. Process is pushed very hard, meanings emerge. The symbolic hierarchies of silver and gold are not overlooked – for both must undergo the exact same process. The piece entitled "Collection" consists of shards and scraps of castings precisely because they are of gold – an altogether daring and insouciant contradiction.

△ **Neckpiece "Paar – Mann und Fernseher" (Pair – Man and TV). Andrea Wippermann.** Silver, opal, gold and titanium chain. Cast. 9 cm (3½ in). 1998

Ring. Andrea Wippermann. Gold, silver. Cast. Height 4.5 cm (1¾ in). 1995

⬡ **Neckpiece "Sammlung" (Collection). Andrea Wippermann.** Gold, titanium. Cast. Height 18 cm (7 in). 1997

⬡ **Neckpiece "Paar – im Gespräch" (Pair – in Conversation). Andrea Wippermann.** Silver, moonstone, steel rope. Cast. Height 8 cm (3¼ in). 1997

In her series of necklaces, Cynthia Cousens deploys a pictorial vocabulary which is informed and animated by nature study.

Explorations of winter landscapes, with misty fields, hedges and bare branches, with twists and thread-like trails, have led directly from drawings on paper to drawings in metal. The complex lines and forms of skeletal nature provide Cousens with a rich vein of ideas for working wire, and also encourage an un-precious use of silver. Following the natural inclinations of the material itself, she captures the wintry atmosphere with a wide range of greys and blacks, by oxidizing the metal to graphite shades, or even occasionally burning it away, to tease out the brown or pink hues of winter. Rhythmic lines with varying articulation and random formation complete the picture.

With the body movement of the wearer, the long chains – worn either in front or across the shoulder – appear like fragile twigs blown in the wind.

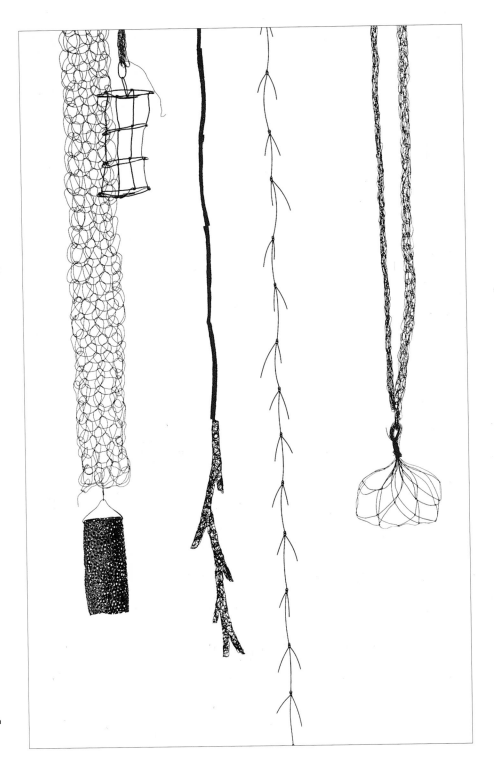

Necklaces from the Winter Series. Cynthia Cousens. Silver. Oxidized. Length 98 - 187 cm (38¼ - 74 in). 1996

The concepts for Esther Knobel's jewellery are incidental and only evolved during the actual working process, in a kind of free development. Preliminary sketches are redundant in this process, which is direct – materials and techniques drive and give shape to form and concept.

An effect of this process is one of contrasting styles in her work. Knobel's earlier pieces have included experiments in differing metals, vivid colours, pattern and rhythmic sequence; often toy-like and generally with a characteristic raw simplicity. Here, inspired by the beauty of nature and elements of the natural world, the "Rose Petal" and "Chinaberry" necklaces are free-modelled and random in their ornament.

Knobel's jewellery makes no claim to symbolism except that in her exploration of materials and process, she succeeds in finding equivalences of nature and that in her selection and manipulation of provisional forms, she finds expression for our fragile foothold in the world. In this respect her pieces give out eloquent messages.

⬙ **Rose Petal Necklace (no.1). Esther Knobel.**
Silver, laminated rose petals. Length approx. 100 cm (39½ in). 1995

⬙ **"Chinaberry" Pendant. Esther Knobel.**
Enamel on copper. Length 16 cm (6¼ in). 1998

Winfried Krüger finds a soft poetry in rough process. His architectonic constructions tease out ambiguous expressions from two of the most fundamental of metalwork and jewellery craft technologies – assemblage and casting.

Brooch. Winfried Krüger. Turquoise, cameo, onyx, lapis, amethyst, moss agate. Cast from sunflower head. Ø 9 cm (3½ in). 1996

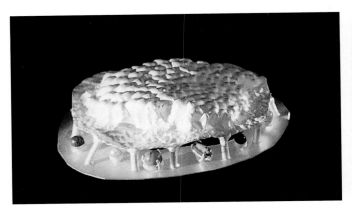

Ring "Well". Winfried Krüger. Silver, topaz. Cast. 5.5 x 2.5 cm (2¼ x 1 in). 1996

Krüger exposes and delights in the archaic resonances of the process, turning artifice, cultural and technological development against themselves, recovering through his simple ornamentations the primitive impulse to bejewel. His awkward, hesitant combinations of form re-enact that sense of magic and wonder with which the emergent metal object is retrieved from its mould, the preciousness of the moment, and a transformation that is precious and wondrous in itself.

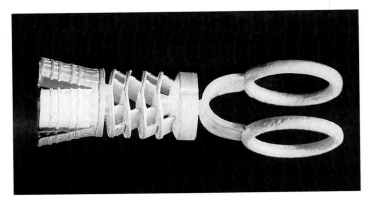

Ring "Chasseur". Winfried Krüger. Silver. Cast. Length 9 cm (3½ in), Ø 2.5 cm (1 in). 1997

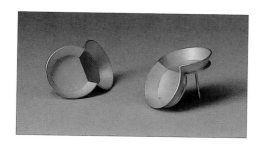

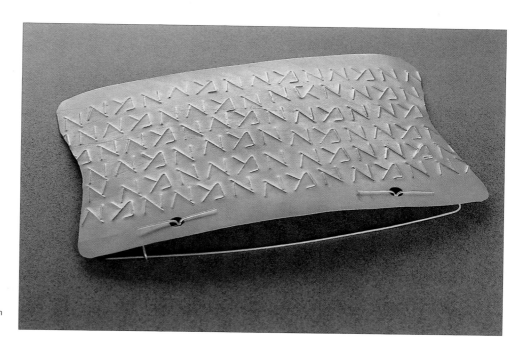

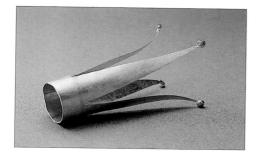

Two Cones – Earrings. Noam Elyashiv. 18ct gold. Constructed. 2.5 x 1.5 x 0.7 cm (1 x ⅝ x ¼ in). 1998

Noam Elyashiv works with the aesthetic of sheet metal. Simple and modest interventions permit its voice to speak quietly, but persuasively, across centuries.

IMA (Mother) Brooch. Noam Elyashiv. Silver. Embossed. 9 x 15 cm (3½ x 6 in). 1992

Crown Ring. Noam Elyashiv. Silver, turquoise. Constructed. 2 x 7 cm (¾ x 2¾ in). 1992

Nothing here is forced, there is no cleverness and no sense of the author. The expression is unmodern. A ring is cut and wrapped around, earrings simply fabricated, a brooch inscribed with cuneiform markings. The pervading sense is of relaxed restraint, tempered by a joy in plain expression – so much can be achieved by so little. Let the metal work, why push harder? The resonances are completely coherent. The pieces achieve a dry, archeological, out-of-the-sand, biblical sonority – simplicity and conviction make all the right connections.

Ring. Mizuko Yamada. Silver. Forged and soldered.
3 x 4.5 x 4 cm (1¼ x 1¾ x 1½ in). 1998

*Mizuko Yamada is a tremendously skilful maker of hollow forms
in metal.*

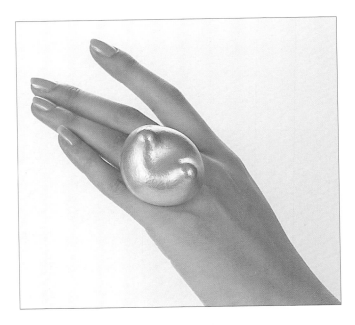

*She endows the metal with a softness which contradicts its nature as it
denies the intense concentration and dexterity with which it has been
hammered into shape from the original flat sheet. The forms tenderly
teased out, with great finesse, pull back just this side of erotic, remaining
as surreal abstractions: clouds, containers, dreams, sometimes a little
macabre – with the tight sheen of improbability.*

These strange objects are in the world, but not quite of it.

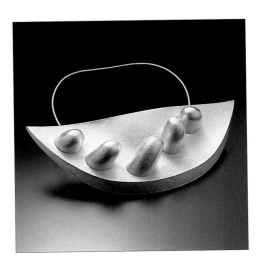

Breast Ornament. Mizuko Yamada. Silver-plated
copper. Forged and soldered. 7.5 x 43 x 35 cm
(3 x 17 x 13¾ in). 1994

Three Rings. Mizuko Yamada. Silver. Forged and
soldered. Left to right: 7 x 4.5 x 4.5 cm;
6.5 x 6.5 x 5.5 cm; 6.5 x 7 x 4 cm
(2¾ x 1¾ x 1¾ in/2½ x 2½ x 2¼ in/2½ x 2¾ x 1¾ in).
1994

🔺 **Ring. Mizuko Yamada.** Silver-plated copper. Forged and soldered.
10.5. 8 x 8 cm (4¼ x 3¼ x 3¼ in). 1998

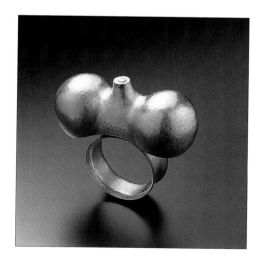

🔺 **Bracelet (no.6). Mizuko Yamada.** Silver-plated
copper. Forged, soldered and welded.
11 x 17 x 18 cm (4¼ x 6¾ x 7 in). 1992

🔺 **Bracelet (no.5). Mizuko Yamada.** Silver-plated
copper. Forged and welded. 12.5 x 6 x 13.5 cm
(5 x 2¼ x 5¼ in). 1992

Christoph Zellweger has a very sharp eye for the qualities of materials and for the the most telling details of formal expression.

Emerging from within the classic goldsmithing tradition, Zellweger has sought to situate his artistic production in opposition to it, determined to integrate or temper his instinct for the precious with materials which are, paradoxically, quintessentially base. Nevertheless, he approaches each new material with respect and finesse.

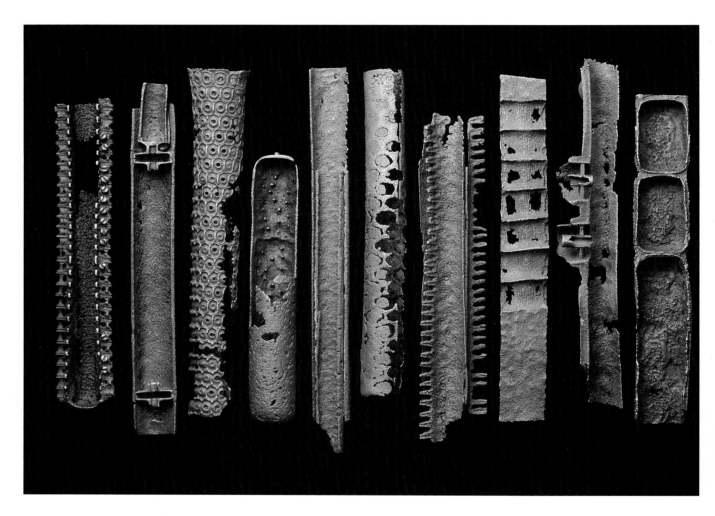

His finely cast steel brooches wring the last ounce of expression from that process. He has worked at the edge of its limitations to produce a series of objects which betray no craftsmanship but are absorbing in their patterns of eloquent decay. They appear as the discovered, ambiguous remains of artefacts which have lain in some corrosive slurry, mute testimonies to forgotten and obsolete purposes.

◯ **Brooches.**
Christoph Zellweger.
Mild steel, stainless steel. Ceramic shell casting. 14 - 18 cm (5½ - 7 in). 1993-1995

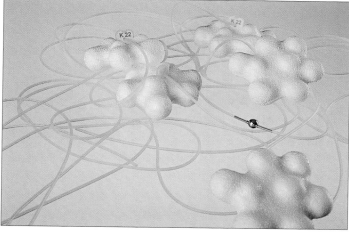

△ **Chain (detail). Christoph Zellweger.** Mild steel, latex. Ceramic shell casting, hand-fabricated latex tubes. Length 300 cm (118 in). 1994

△ **Commodity Chain k22. Christoph Zellweger.** Polystyrene, plastic, silicon tubes, chrome-plated silver. Polystyrene expanded in hand-fabricated metal moulds. 200 x 400 cm (79 x 157½ in), elements approx. Ø 6 cm (2½ in). 1998

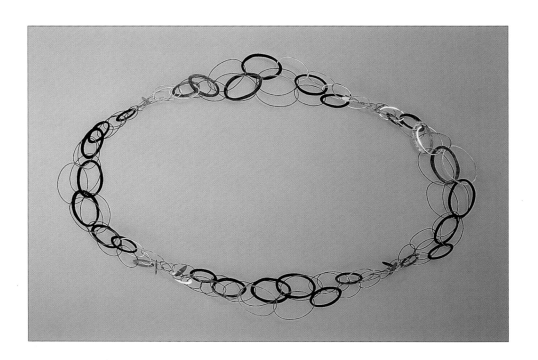

36

Simplicity and clarity define the
techniques applied by Annelies
Planteydt.

Visual effects are created by varying
coloured metals, such as gold and
tantalum, in a random combination.
Her necklaces of multi-shaped linear
outlines alternate with diverse spatial
elements to produce an optical illusion
of movement – a theme found
throughout Planteydt's jewellery.

For her, form is flexible, and through its
repetitions forms a natural ornament. In
fact, the necklaces provide a basis,
enabling her to experiment with
differing possibilities of dimensions,
structure and animation. When worn,
the element of movement is intensified
by the body's motion.

Ovals – Necklace. Annelies Planteydt.
Tantalum, 18 ct gold, 24 ct gold. All parts
connected and hammered on tension. 38 x
25 cm (15 x 10 in). 1996

**The Travelling Woman – Necklace.
Annelies Planteydt.** Tantalum, 18ct gold.
All parts connected and hammered on
tension. 45 x 20 cm (18 in x 8 in). 1998

Jacqueline Ryan's work reveals a profound attachment to nature and an instinctive alliance with ancient goldsmithing.

She is fascinated by the readiness with which gold, in paper-thin sheets, can be persuaded to represent the most delicate petals, leaves and seeds. Her insistent and loving repetition of many small parts, their fragility and their animation by tiny movements, reinforces her message that the most modest, delicate and often unnoticed flowers are also the most beautiful.

Pendant. Jacqueline Ryan. 18ct gold and enamels. Made up of approx. 400 movable enamelled parts. Ø 6 cm (2¼ in). 1996

Brooch. Jacqueline Ryan. 18ct gold and enamels. Made up of numerous movable enamelled parts. Ø 6 cm (2¼ in). 1996

Ring. Jacqueline Ryan. 18ct gold. Made up of movable parts. 3 x 2 x 2.5 cm (1¼ in x ¾ in x 1 in). 1997

The colours and materials with which Ryan augments gold, whilst consonant with nature, are also redolent of ancient jewellery – turquoise, coral, pearl – so that she simultaneously represents the natural world she sees and establishes a link with the past of her art: a romantic association, which is very convincingly done.

These are powerful, challenging pieces, which stand at once outside and within jewellery convention.

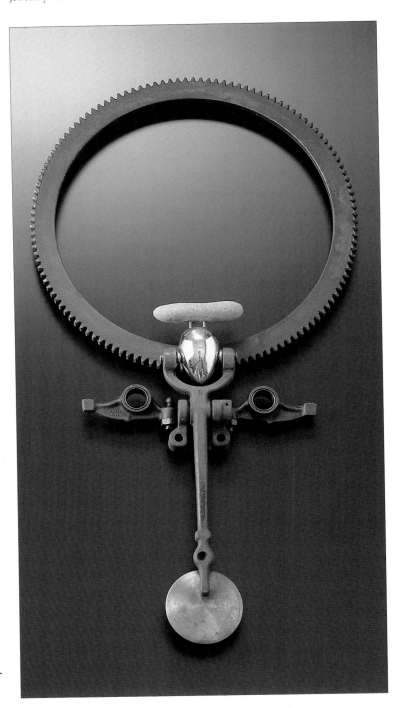

Regenerat. Wahei Ikezawa.
Stone, iron, brass. Assembled.
60 x 33 cm (23 x 13 in). 1994

They are very large and composed of tough, even brutal elements. These clearly relate to devices and machines which were formerly harnessed to utility and force. They are now incorporated into the proud and ancient form of a pendant or body piece. They are to some extent denatured and humanized by the incorporation but they also remain disquietlingly apart, totemic.

⬗ **Sacred. Wahei
Ikezawa.** Rope, brass,
stainless, copper.
Assembled. 50 x
24 cm (19½ x 9½ in).
1990

*Ikezawa concentrates on the rich and varied expressive qualities and resonances of the materials
he selects. His skill is in binding them together in tight compositions, to provide his own
structure to the borrowed elements.*

Sonia Morel's chain mail rings are evidence of a process played out unremittingly: the objects becoming unnaturally dense – thickets of form and materials – the meaning grows out of the process. They are very elaborate and intricate structures into which moving elements are added, having either a decorative function or an association with body armour. In one, small sheets of metal cover the inner ring and become a carapace to guard the wearer. Another with an organic form has particles forming a veil over the ring itself, the whole made to look like a tree, with suspended silver globules as ripe fruit. A playful aspect becomes apparent in her designs, as in the ring covered with mobile disc-like links, which when worn swing from side to side and caress the hand.

 **Silver Ring.
Sonia Morel.** Silver.
Ring skeleton with
metallic links hung
in suspension.
5.5 x 4 x 4 cm
(2 x 1½ x 1½ in).
1997

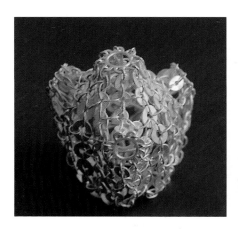

**Silver Ring.
Sonia Morel.** Oxidized
silver. 5.5 x 4.5 x
4.5 cm (2⅛ x 1¾ x
1¾ in). 1997

**Silver Ring.
Sonia Morel.** Silver.
Ring with an armour
of interlinked flat
sheets.
3.5 x 3.5 x 5 cm
(1⅜ x 1⅜ x 2 in).
1997

**Silver Ring.
Sonia Morel.** Oxidized
silver. Little silver
globes on a
framework attached
to the ring.
4.5 x 3.5 x 3 cm
(1¾ x 1⅜ x 1¼ in).
1997

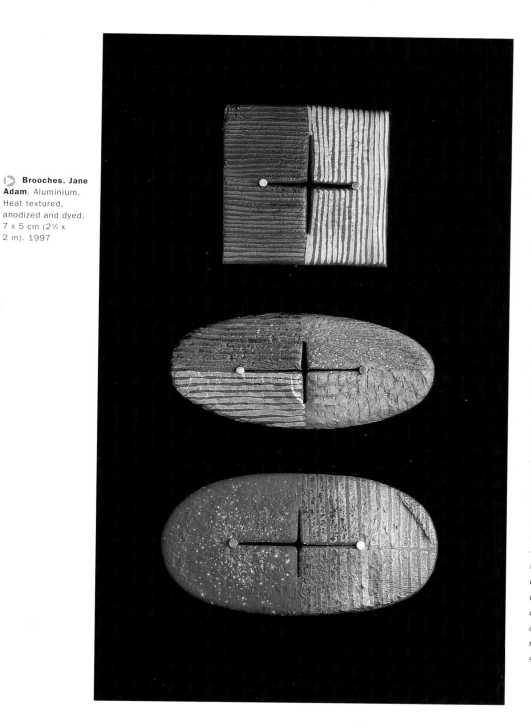

Brooches. Jane Adam. Aluminium. Heat textured, anodized and dyed. 7 x 5 cm (2¾ x 2 in). 1997

Jane Adam has developed an extraordinary expertise in the technique and art of decorating metals through anodizing aluminium.

The use of aluminium in itself poses interesting and non-traditional problems for the artist jeweller. Unlike precious metals, for instance, it is not easily soldered, which therefore demands ingenuity in attaching fittings. The material can be beautiful in itself, but is strongly associated with commercial, non-jewellery product, and there is the challenge.

The industrial method of colouring aluminium involves the development of a hard oxide surface, which is dyed by dipping parts or complete objects in large tanks. Adam has claimed this process for the jewellery maker through years of experiment, not as an academic researcher but as a working designer-maker. She has introduced a complexity, through a range of direct techniques including mark making, which far exceeds our expectation of this everyday commercial process, and has acquired a depth of knowledge about its phenomena which results in very rich colours, surfaces and effects.

41

▽ **Necklace. Nel
Linssen.** Paper. Folded
circular shapes, turned on
elastic tube. 3.8 x
20.3 cm (1½ x 8 in).
1995

◇ **Necklace.
Nel Linssen.** Paper.
Circular shapes on elastic
tube. 3.5 x 19 cm
(1⅜ in x 7½ in). 1995

◀ *Paper is a beautiful material, full of paradoxical properties. We all know it well through eyes and fingers, yet rarely pause to consider what a precious cultural artefact it is. Nel Linssen is a connoisseur.*

Her approach has been to treat individual pieces of paper as beads, piling them up into soft, seductive forms whose gravity overcomes their flimsiness. She assembles them so as to produce rolling algebraic forms of precisely articulated profiles and, further, intertwining chains and gradations of colour. In such ways, she demonstrates that simplicity and repetition will generate complexity and resolution.

Many contemporary jewellers have explored the potential of paper as a medium, but few have matched the singular coherence of Linssen's vision.

Ring. Etsuko Sonobe. 835 gold, pearl. Set. 28 x 14 x 22 cm (11 x 5½ x 8¾ in). 1997

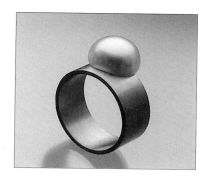

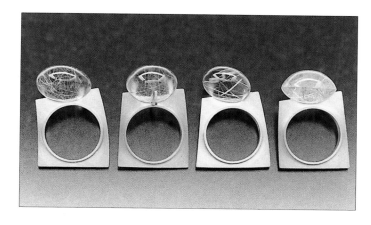

Rings. Etsuko Sonobe. 835 gold, rutilated quartz. Cut stone. 32 x 22 x 15 cm (12½ x 8¾ x 6 in). 1998

The jewellery of Etsuko Sonobe has true grace and modesty. Underlying its apparent simplicity is the supple strength of a moral dimension.

Sonobe is above all respectful of her materials, seeking only to enhance their beauty, to achieve a balance between their inner nature and their given form. Stones and metal are brought together simply, transparently, directly, so that they speak clearly of an accommodation between the hand of nature and the hand of the maker. She achieves a harmony between the material and the method.

In this case the maker has a moral position, acting not passively but as a guide, seeking sympathetic forms and junctions which will resolve the constituent parts into expressive unities. There is, however, no superfluous gesture, no trickery, no intrusive ego, nothing to deflect the eye from the simple beauty of the materials. These are her articles of faith.

It is a very persuasive and quietly authoritative demonstration.

Esther Ward's fascination with the linked rod-and-eye method of construction is complete. Superficially, there is no more simple, more economical, more pure method of creating a necklace. It is a kind of constructional plain speaking. This is an attractively disingenuous starting point which nevertheless contains a certain moral assurance. Out of such simplicity can come more complex motives, teasing ambiguities. And this dualism is, one suspects, what keeps Esther running.

She has explored the possibilities of the form at length and with great inventiveness. Her constructions have revealed how minute alterations to the geometry of the single joint will, when repeated and combined, cause surprising expansions into light and airy structures. She has combined metals, including precious metals, for their colours, but has generally returned to uncomplicated stainless steel, which she treats with great respect.

Ward enjoys the dualism of fluidity and angularity which the form confers, the way in which, by repetition, spidery, almost weightless elements assume substance on the body, the way implicitly machine-like repetition is subtly nuanced by hand making. The sensuous pleasure of making is as evident as the honest simplicity of method.

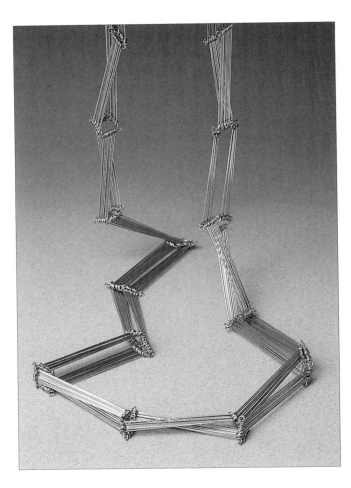

◇ **Straight Ribbon Necklace. Esther Ward.**
Stainless steel.
Fabricated wire. Hanging
length 30 cm (12 in).
1995

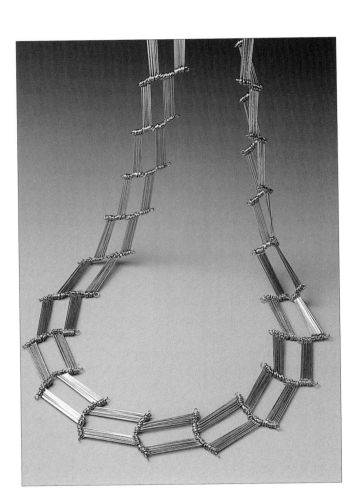

◇ **Double Harlequin Neckpiece. Esther Ward.**
Stainless steel.
Fabricated wire. Hanging
length 30 cm (12 in).
1998

Tablewear.
Gerlinde Huth.
Goldplated brass.
Sheet fabrication. Left
to right: 8 x 8 x 2.5
cm; 6.5 x 4 x 2.5 cm;
7.5 x 4.5 x 2.5 cm; 6
x 6 x 2.5 cm (3¼ x 3¼
x 1 in; 2½ x 1½ x 1in;
3 x 1¾ x 1 in; 2¼ x 2¼
x 1 in). 1995

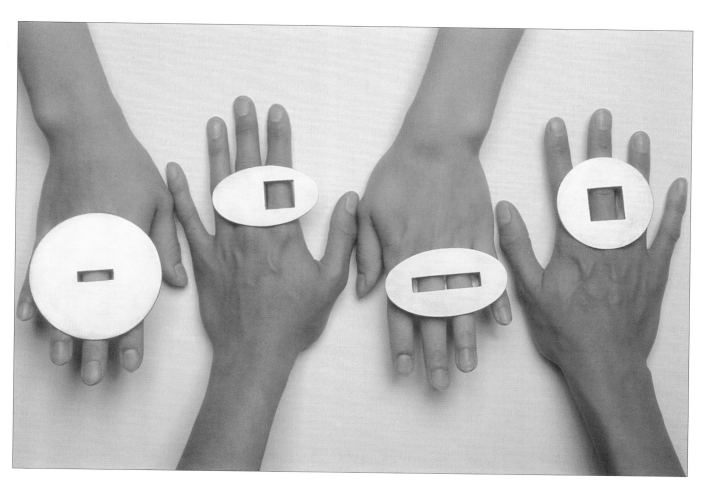

Gerlinde Huth's big eye-catching rings flash in the light like golden masks or shields. Ambiguously modern yet in their plainness archaic, Bauhaus in lineage, at once perfect and primitive, with interplay of the simplest geometries conditional on the position of fingers, their soft surfaces nevertheless resonate to a distant theatre of swords and daggers, buckles and sashes.

Huth's idea seems modest but her resolution is complex in its effect. These are very fine rings. They guarantee moments of real drama to the confident gesture of expressive hands. Gold, in the right hands, on the right hands, can do that.

The jewellery of Felicity Peters, modest and undemonstrative in form, is however imbued with a presence which is at once difficult to pin down, yet real. Its voice is soft and reverent, its meanings mysterious.

The tone of reverence is in some way coupled to the very process of craft. The work illuminates the fact that for some artists the fine and sensitive working of metal provides a direct conduit to other realms of feeling and understanding – to connection with nature, the past, to dreams and memories.

The sense of mystery is compounded by the care lavished on these objects, and by their relative simplicity, but especially it derives from their small scale, resonating as they do with myth, prayer and ritual.

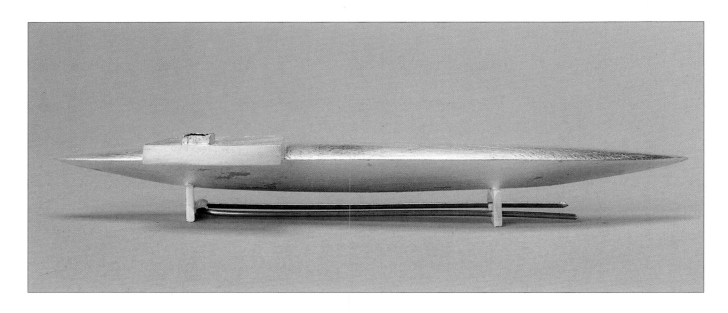

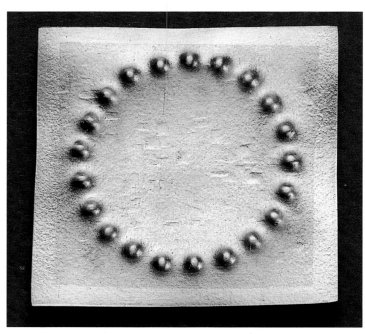

▷ **When the Bubble Bursts (brooch). Felicity Peters.**
Sterling silver, 24 ct gold keum boo. Hammered, roller printed, repoussé, keum boo.
5.7 x 5.4 cm (2⅛ x 2⅛ in).
1997

△ **Journey Boat Brooch Green Light. Felicity Peters.**
Sterling silver, 24 ct gold keum boo, tourmaline. Formed, constructed, keum boo.
9 x 1.9 (widest part) x 1.5 cm (3½ x ¾ x ⅝ in). 1996

Shiang-shin Yeh shows work which reveals fascination with the phenomena of order and structure.

There are no "stories", no overt "biographies" here. Implicit in the carefully restrained interplay and interpenetration of shape and surface of these objects is the conviction that pure order, harmoniously expressed, will communicate on some deeper level than that of narrative – what Yeh calls "harmonic mood".

There is something akin to a musical experience about these structures, again, not lyrical but in the repetition of complex motifs and in the projection of tonal values which are strange in their dark purity. Play on numbers and their relationships connects to man's fascination with them in both nature and the intellect, and we can easily empathize with the artist's meditative absorption in the discipline of making.

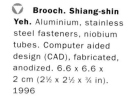

Brooch. Shiang-shin Yeh. Aluminium, stainless steel fasteners, niobium tubes. Computer aided design (CAD), fabricated, anodized. 6.6 x 6.6 x 2 cm (2½ x 2½ x ¾ in). 1996

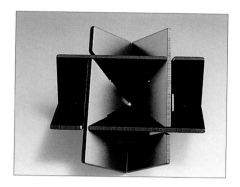

Brooch. Shiang-shin Yeh. Aluminium, stainless steel fasteners, niobium tubes. Computer aided design (CAD), fabricated, anodized. 7.3 x 7.3 x 1.8 cm (3 x 3 x ¾ in). 1996

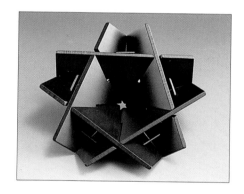

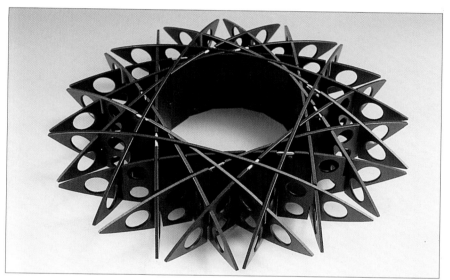

Bracelet. Shiang-shin Yeh. Aluminium, spring bars. Computer aided design (CAD), fabricated, anodized. 18 x 18 x 4 cm (7 x 7 x 1½ in). 1996

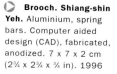

Brooch. Shiang-shin Yeh. Aluminium, spring bars. Computer aided design (CAD), fabricated, anodized. 7 x 7 x 2 cm (2¾ x 2¾ x ¾ in). 1996

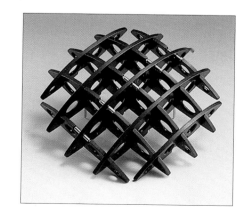

47

Ring. Dongchun Lee.
Iron. Sawn and welded.
7 x 8.6 x 1.8 cm
(2¾ x 3¼ x ¾ in). 1996

Ring. Dongchun Lee.
Iron, iron-wire. Sawn.
9 x 5.5 x 0.5 cm
(3½ x 2⅛ x ¼ in). 1996

Dongchun Lee favours iron as a medium for his jewellery, and he finds an unusual method for applying this metal - he saws, bends and welds, to achieve an etched-in-space quality.

He celebrates its traditional identity as a symbol of force and strength. Its mysterious blackness has an almost incomprehensible secretive depth, as in our innermost thoughts.

In essence, Lee's outstandingly sculptural jewellery is a personal expression. His preliminary ink drawings – which we can clearly sense from the character of the jewellery – echo his inner voice, and the expressive outlines explode with gestures and emotions. The forms are full of movement and life.

Such sculptural objects, worn on the body, enhance the beauty of the wearer and simultaneously become communicative forms.

Silke Trekel's striking and sombrely luxuriant, lightweight neckpieces, of balsa wood, paper and paint, are unique in a Western context. Their inspiration appears to derive in part from the arts and crafts of China but they also show great originality.

Trekel's works are complete and beautifully resolved examples of the transference of values from precious to non-precious materials. By the work of her hand the inherent beauty of the materials is thereby revealed, to be discovered, shared and appreciated.

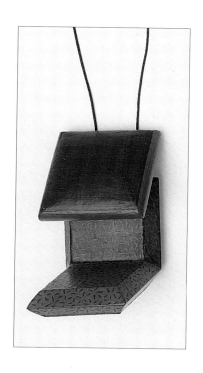

Neckpiece. Silke Trekel. Balsa wood. Laminated and painted. Height 11 cm (4¼ in). 1997

Neckpiece. Silke Trekel. Balsa wood. Laminated and painted. 30 cm (12 in). 1997

**Wisteria Necklace.
Charlotte de Syllas.**
Jadeite jade and silk.
Carved beads from solid
jade using diamond hand
tools and boride stone.
approx. 43 cm (17 in)
long. 1995

◄ *Charlotte de Syllas treats every piece she makes as an aesthetic and technical challenge.*

She selects her materials carefully, with a sensitive eye for their intrinsic qualities, and works them slowly and painstakingly to achieve her sculpted ideal. Her technique of choice is carving, which she does only with hand files, eschewing machinery in favour of direct, subjective control – of which she shows great command. As a result her pieces have a strong sense of having been worked over, the expressed precision of hand and eye alone, their fullness of form achieved by the smallest of incremental stages.

The combination of carved jadeite and braided silk is quite typical, the silk being braided by her collaborator Catherine Martin – another artist who works, in her own highly developed technique, to demanding and exacting standards.

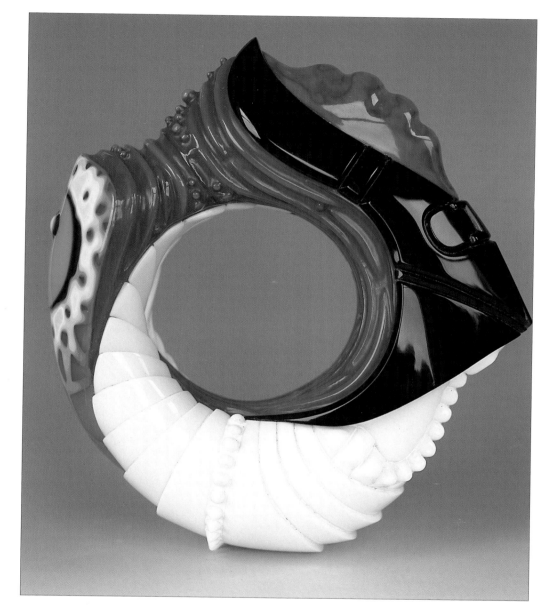

○ **Bracelet. Peter Chang.** Acrylic and polyester, lacquerwork. Carved, thermo-formed, lathe-turned. Ø 15 cm (6 in). thickness 6 cm (2¼ in) . 1996

The fashionable and witty jewels of Peter Chang, in vibrant colours and in a kaleidoscope of ornament, have established a unique and compelling presence in the contemporary jewellery field.

Chang creates not only imperishable but also precious objects from materials which are normally used for throw-away products and even from recycled elements.

These are complex constructions which combine a variety of techniques in working the many different plastics – acrylic, PVC, polyurethane and others – which reflect the age we live in. Chang's training as a sculptor and his experiments in furniture-making are evident in his jewellery, which has a distinctly sculptural quality and a large scale, but the key expression is of elaborate shapes, with animated forms and ornate patterns. The results are full of energy and clamour, not crude but worked with intensity and exactitude, the opaque and translucent application of multi-layered plastics giving the illusion of, and reference to, precious lacquerwork.

Gerda Flöckinger's baroque forms and highly developed technique of precious metal fusion are instantly recognizable to jewellery lovers in Great Britain, where she has enjoyed an outstanding reputation for many years.

She works her chosen material dangerously close to the point of disintegration in pursuit of its enrichment, scattering precious and semi-precious stones as if in metallic larva. The effect is ambiguously modern, at once natural and contrived, betraying a sophisticated eye for form coupled with the instinctive acknowledgement of a cultured opulence.

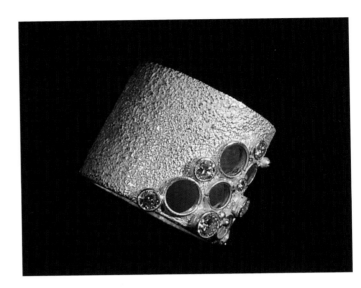

Ring. Gerda Flöckinger. 18ct gold, golden diamonds. Fusion. 1.6 x 1.8 cm (⅝ x ¾ in). 1997

52

Bracelet. Gerda Flöckinger. 18ct gold, cabochon amethyst fastening, pink, lilac, grey, brown, beige and dark diamonds, cultured white and blue pearls. Fusion. Bracelet: length 18 cm (7 in); tails length 9 cm (3½ in). 1994

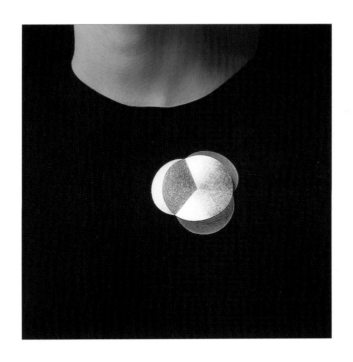

Brooch. Castello Hansen. Silver. Gilded, constructed from sheet. Width 7 cm (2¾ in). 1997

Castello Hansen harnesses unusual technique to the task of enrichment: perhaps "enhancement" would be more accurate. His purpose is to make the gold appear more intensely golden. He achieves this through effects by which surface form can trap and reflect light.

Hansen is a fine and sensitive goldsmith. He has a musician's appreciation for the alliance of precision and nuance, and an idealist's commitment to the resonance of perfect form.

The forms are reminiscent of religious or mythical symbols. If it is not too fanciful an interpretation, Hansen's ambition is to discover some timeless current within jewellery – one through which his work will connect to the head waters of ancient traditions. If it is so, this is a wonderful ambition.

Gold Disc Necklace. Castello Hansen. Acrylic gold leaf, oxydized silver, rubber. Turned, carved. Width 19 cm (7½ in). 1996

PROCESS, POETRY & MEANING

Catherine Hills works her metal hard. Her primary concerns are the interplay of positive and negative through form and colour.

Group of Necklaces, Brooch and Ring. **Catherine Hills.** Oxidized silver, 18ct gold, blue glass, red resin and C2 stone and painted enamel. Large pressed hollow forms, fly pressed, soldered and inlaid. Smallest: 3 cm (1¼ in) wide; largest: 9 cm (3½ in) wide. 1992-3

Her pieces are also, incidentally, images of many or plenty, metaphors for creative productivity and the iterative process – achieving understanding and increasing command of the medium by making and making. Hills apparently likes to see a lot of it, to worry away at it, to test every variation on a theme, coaxing nuances of tone, rhythm and form through subtleties of surface treatment, oxidization, interval, piercing and shaping. The possibilities are never-ending.

Some jewellers are excited by creative productivity itself – are driven by it. Hills is probably one of them.

◑ **Large Round Earrings with Detachable Snowdrop Studs. Catherine Hills.** Oxidized silver, silver, 24ct goldplated silver. Cast. Ø 2 cm (¾ in). 1998

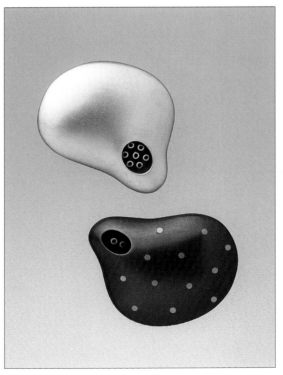

◑ **Two Amoeba Brooches. Catherine Hills.** Matt silver, oxidized silver, 18 ct gold. Fly-pressed and inlaid. 3·5cm (1⅜ in). 1997

Elizabeth Bone is a fine and confident professional, representing a growing band of young designer makers who are developing and feeding a broad emergent market for individualistic jewellery.

Bone's work is epitomized by caring craftsmanship and subdued elegance. Scale, unforced geometry, classic techniques and sensitive surfaces project a cool modesty. There is little evidence of the artist's ego, no biography, no "issues". Except perhaps to express the thought that within such a frame of restraint and understatement the metal itself, gently encouraged to speak of its own soft beauty, becomes a receptacle for the wearer, and so awaits the warmth of ownership.

△ **Necklace. Elizabeth Bone.** Silver. Folded sheet. Length approx. 116 cm (45¾ in). 1997-8

◁ **Brooch. Elizabeth Bone.** Silver with 22ct gold leaf detail, steel pin. Fabricated sheet, cast shapes. Ø 5.7 cm (2¼ in). 1997

Anne Finlay's jewellery is in some ways the most redolent of the "alternative jewellery" movement of the early eighties. The continuance and evolution of her work, in which she typically combines playful and structural elements to create an imaginative whole, is a tribute to the clear vision which has guided it.

A variety of geometric shapes, segments and lines, made of either hand-painted or screen-printed PVC are connected by fine stainless steel wires and rubber elements. The flexible parts are die-cut before being assembled. Red, yellow and blue are the primary colours which she applies in combination with black, and on rare occasions with white. Colour and pattern predominate in her jewellery, and with a few recurring elements she infers an inconceivable number of solutions.

Finlay has shown that with inexpensive materials, wearable art objects in good designs are affordable.

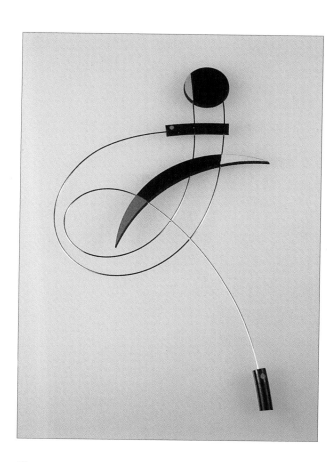

△ **Brooch. Anne Finlay.** PVC, stainless steel wire, rubber. Machine-cut, hand-painted. 9 x 17 cm (3½ x 6¾ in). 1997

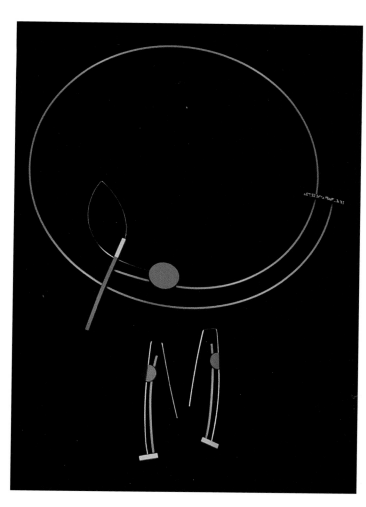

△ **Neckpiece and Earrings. Anne Finlay.** PVC, nylon, stainless steel wire. Machine- and hand-cut, die-cut, screen printed. 26 x 23 cm (10¼ x 9 in) and 8 x 1.2 cm (3¼ x ½ in). 1998

Brooch. Joël Degen. 18ct gold sheet, stainless steel sheet, titanium, stainless steel screws. Polished, semi-matt finished. (The brooch is made of several parts held together with 4 small stainless steel screws.) 6 x 6 cm (2¼ x 2¼ in). 1998

Ring. Joël Degen. 18ct gold square wire, titanium, gold, stainless steel. Satin-finished. (The ring is made up of four separate elements held together with stainless steel as well as gold rivets.) 2.2 x 0.6 cm (¾ x ¼ in). 1993

Four Rings. Joël Degen. Emerald, ruby, 18ct gold, titanium, stainless steel. File-finished. (Each ring is held together with 6 long stainless steel rivets, the stones are trapped rather than set.) 2.2 x 1 cm (¾ x ⅜ in). 1996

Joël Degen's aesthetic is, essentially, constructed, the clean lines and cool surfaces contributing to a general air of modernity.

Degen uses a combination of traditional and more contemporary industrial materials – gold and semi-precious stones allied with stainless steel and titanium – all controlled, muted to the point of neutral, unshowy coherence. He produces such pieces in small batches, using ingenious and unorthodox construction techniques. These are not thrust forward for admiration of "workmanship" or "creativity" but may be quietly appreciated within restrained compositional schemes.

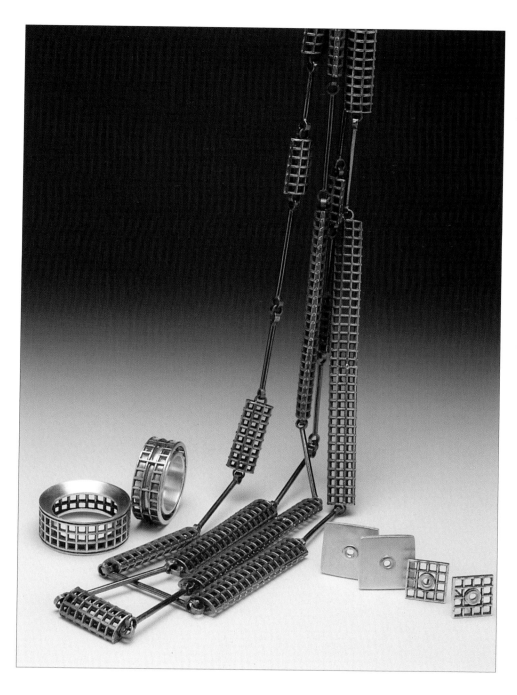

● **Necklace, Rings and Earrings. Noon Mitchelhill.** Silver and gold. Cast mesh, other pieces hand-fabricated. Necklace length: 102 cm (41 in); rings: 2.5 x 2.5 x 1 cm (1 x 1 x ⅜ in), earrings: 1.5 x 1.5 cm (⅝ x ⅝ in). 1997. 1998

Noon Mitchelhill makes jewellery which is often complex in its construction but simple in its intentions.

This jewellery is absolutely for wearing. Her work explores richness in texture and subtlety of colour; it speaks of the pleasure of making, of repetition, of nuance, articulation and counterchange; it is expressly hand-made. She clearly enjoys working in metals, especially silver, and produces uncomplicated pieces which allow others to appreciate the basic elements.

Rings. Kirsten Garzareck. 925 silver, emeralds, rubies, tourmaline, sapphires. Assembled. Height 5 cm (2 in). 1996

Ring. Kirsten Garzareck. 925 silver, teavorites. Hand-cast. Length 6 cm (2¼ in). 1997

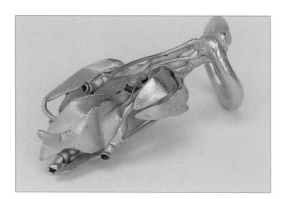

Ring. Kirsten Garzareck. 925 silver, synthetic stone. Hand-cast. Height 6 - 7 cm (2¼ - 2¾ in). 1997

Ring. Kirsten Garzareck. Gilded 925 silver, synthetic stones. Hand-cast. Height 6 cm (2¼ in). 1997

Kirsten Garzareck demonstrates an outstanding feeling for the modelled surface in metal and for the disorder of natural forms.

The vision seems not yet fully resolved, its focus unclear, and perhaps that is the point, for the working method is opportunistic, one of intuitive handling. The search is for a uniquely expressive moment of the translation of soft wax directly to hard metal. The results are effortlessly tangible and acquire a real sculptural force and authority.

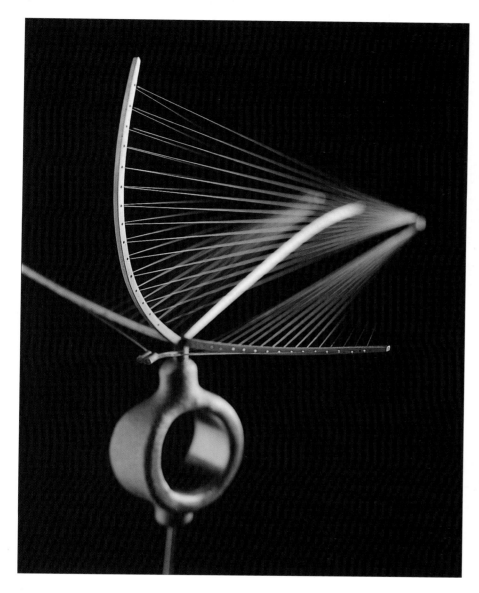

⬤ **Ring. Tomasz Ogrodowski.** Silver, nylon thread. Silver base cast from potato. 11 x 9 cm (4¼ x 3¾ in. 1997

⬤ **Two rings. Tomasz Ogrodowski.** Silver, synthetic material, nylon thread. Silver bases cast from potato. 8 x 8.5 cm (3⅛ x 3¼ in; 10 x 8.5 cm (4 x 3¼ in). 1997

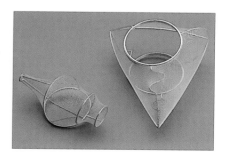

⬤ **Bracelet and Brooch. Tomasz Ogrodowski.** Silver, synthetic material. Bracelet: 11 x 6 cm (4¼ x 2¼); brooch: 4 x 4 cm (1⅝ x 1⅝ in). 1997

Tomasz Ogrodowski's jewels are clearly sculptural in their ambition, his wire frame forms crossing between present-day surface modelling and the kinetic constructivism of the early years of the century, the works as a whole affecting a dynamic between opposing sensibilities.

The contradictions are not simply historical. Two rings in particular derive their current edginess from an ironic juxtaposition between delicate upper forms, of engineered precision, and the curiously massive, lumpen rings from which they spring. In this way their formal expression twitches uncertainly between past and present, between the intellectual and the intuitive.

The jeweller and metalworker, Rudolf Bott, has an
exceptional talent for creating both small and large-scale
objects with expressive sculptural qualities. The brooches
illustrated are distinctly sculptural in intention.

A common, constrained vocabulary of identical forms
appears throughout his work, which ranges from finger
rings carved in rock crystal, through brooches mounted in
gold or brass sheet, hololithic cutlery, to tableware in
bronze and even a table. The dimensions of his pieces and
the techniques applied are interchangeable.

◐ **Brooch. Rudolf
Bott.** 750 yellow gold.
Assembled. 10 x 6 x
3.5 cm (4 x 2¼ x 1⅜
in). 1996

◯ **Brooch. Rudolf Bott.**
750 yellow gold.
Assembled.
10 x 6 x 3.5 cm (4 x 2¼ x
1⅜ in). 1996

Bott experiments with various materials, their
possibilities of expression and the different craft processes
which they require. In his metalcraft, surface treatment is
significant. The viewer can detect how the fundamental
forms in metal or stone are developed out of mass and
volume. The decorative element is reduced to a minimum.

Simplicity and refinement seem to characterize his work,
which appears both archaic and modernist and so is
firmly fixed within a core twentieth century tradition.

Adam Jirkal's jewellery is formed from the simplest, most severe two-dimensional geometries of circle, square and triangle, held in tension.

Within the constraints of these geometries he plays upon the variations of sheet, bar and wire to construct an architecture of planar intersections. The glass, which adds a frisson of danger to the wearability of these objects also exposes, by its transparency, the play of their construction. The theme of intersection lies not only in the internal structure of these objects, but also in their challenging intersection with the softness of the body. The warmth, fullness, tone, strength and vulnerability of flesh will itself be emphasized by their opposing properties.

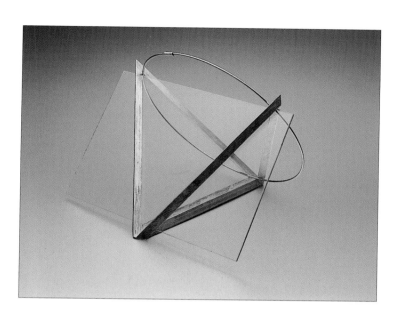

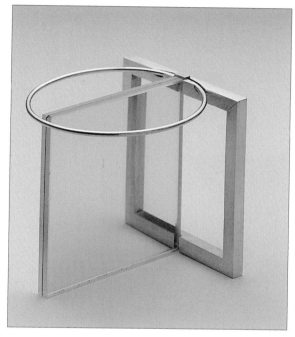

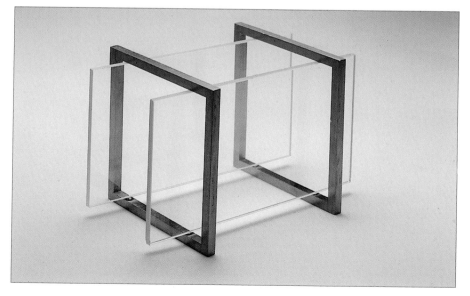

△ **Bracelet. Adam Jirkal.** 925 silver, stainless steel, glass. Fabricated. 10 x 14 x 12 cm (4 x 5½ x 4¾ in). 1995

△ **Ring. Adam Jirkal.** Nickel silver, mirror glass, stainless steel. Fabricated. 4.5 x 4.5 x 4.5 cm (1¾ x 1¾ x 1¾ in). 1996

◒ **Bracelet. Adam Jirkal.** Steel, rubber, glass. Fabricated. 7.5 x 7.5 x 12 cm (3 x 3 x 4¾ in). 1995

Imke Jörns explores the nature of
aluminium through an aesthetic in which
the twin virtues are honesty and raw
directness, and the agenda is most
definitely the representation of unforced
ornament.

○‹ ›› Necklace.
Imke Jörns.
Aluminium. Welded.
Height approx.
35 cm (14 in).
1996

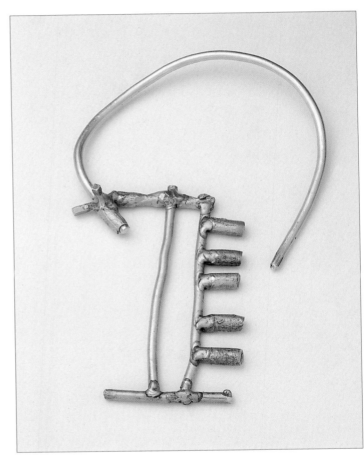

The material is minimally worked and
boldly configured, the basic techniques of
casting, welding and anodizing expressed
without concealment or finesse of
craftsmanship – but not without
artfulness. The wearer participates in the
aesthetic of adornment with a gut
physicality and without extraneous
ornament.

Piece for the
Shoulder. Imke Jörns.
Anodized aluminium. Cast,
soldered, anodized.
30 x 25 cm (12 x 10 in).
1996

PROCESS, POETRY & MEANING

SENSUALITY
& IMAGE

WHETHER FIGURATIVE OR ABSTRACT, jewellery is in essence functional, intended to offer sensuous or physical pleasure or to announce its wearer as a physical, sensuous being. The body is, in effect, its scale, the pysche its domain. The sensation of touch on the body is pre–eminent, but movement and gesture, signal and message also become active participants in a web of visual, physical and psychological elements.

This chapter groups artists who have concentrated their attention on the sensuality of jewellery objects, the capacity of jewellery to express the sensuality of the wearer, and the formal impact of jewellery on the image of the wearer. An artist's aim is truly understood only when the work is worn.

Fluid Forms. Lia de Sain. Steel, foam, epoxy, lacquer. Mixed techniques. Ø 30 cm (12 in). 1995

Fluid Forms: Brooch Thicken Line. Lia de Sain. Steel, foam epoxy and lacquer. Mixed techniques. Length approx. 30 cm (12 in). 1995

Fluid Forms: Necklace Ornament. Lia de Sain. Steel, foam epoxy and lacquer. Mixed techniques. Ø 30 cm (12 in). 1996

Fluid Forms: Necklace Triangle. Lia de Sain. Steel, foam, epoxy and lacquer. Mixed techniques. Ø 30 cm (12 in). 1995

With her "Fluid Form" series of 1995/6, Lia de Sain produced one of the most complete and seductive expressions of the sensuous minimalist aesthetic.

De Sain's work is also a fine example of the modelmaker's art, showing just how far the traditional craft skills of the goldsmith have been invaded, informed and, in some cases, supplanted by more diverse practices. Although the surface build-up of these pieces is reminiscent of ancient lacquerwork, their exaggerated elisions of full form to fine line indicate an infrastructure of steel and modern resins, without which such resolutions would be impossible.

The jewellery offers a certain sensuality in the wearing but the true sensuality of these objects is intrinsic. Their saturated colours and perfect slippery surfaces, their organic but attenuated morphology carries an erotic charge and succinctly expresses the intimacy of the act of their making.

SENSUALITY & IMAGE

**Necklace. Antje
Illner.** Porcelain, silver.
Slip cast. 12.5 x 5 cm
(5 x 2 in). 1997

**Necklace. Antje
Illner.** Porcelain, silver.
Slip cast. 3.8 x 5 cm
(1½ x 2 in). 1997

*Antje Illner's jewellery is remarkable for a tender and intimate eroticism which is
due not only to its forms, but also to the delicate finesse with which she crafts her
chosen materials.*

*Her forms are pared down, generalized, pneumatic, but often, also, attenuated. They
are capable of different interpretations, hovering exquisitely between the literal and
the dreamlike. There is in them a delicate understatement which perfectly expresses, as
it explores, aspects of the private and public realms of jewellery.*

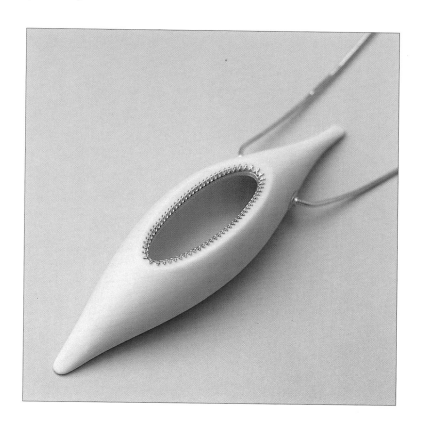

**Necklace. Antje
Illner.** Porcelain, silver.
Slip cast. 14 x 4.5 cm
(5½ x 1¾ in). 1997

Illner has discovered a sympathy for the natural properties of porcelain, so that the forms she has realized are quite unforced and characteristic of its own properties. And yet, in her hands, the outcome is an original and surprising insight of unexpected qualities of warmth and sensuality. This material has become both hard and soft, its forms protectively contained but implicitly fragile. And the metal, which though a simple solution to wearability could so easily overpower its delicate partner, is handled with careful restraint, here and there injecting a perceptible subjective twist.

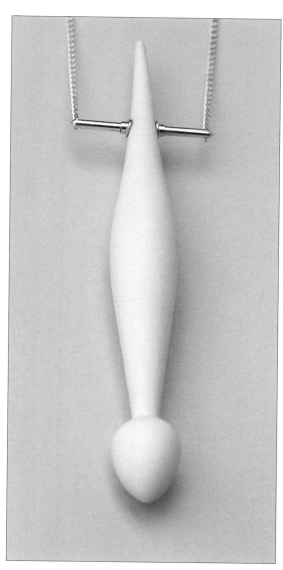

**Necklace. Antje
Illner.** Porcelain, silver.
Slip cast. 15.5 x 2.5 cm
(6 x 1 in). 1997

SENSUALITY & IMAGE

It looks so simple, so domesticated, so banal, this idea of stringing pearl shell buttons. And yet Rowena Gough's results are deeply sensual, the embedded cultural issues complex.

First, it is necessary to understand how these things relate to Oceanic cultures, with their traditions of craft and trade in such materials, to the accumulation and passing on of knowledge and practice through generations, with which the stringing itself makes both literal and metaphorical connections. Then, one must appreciate that the act of threading is at least symbolic of the telling of stories, and, in its intertwining, symbolic of the intermingling of traditions and cultures. It resonates with the cultural loops which carried the pearl button from the Pacific to the West, and back again, with all the political baggage that implies. And the intimacy with which the button relates the many-sided cultural experience of women – their restriction, protection, ornamentation, their labour, deference, tenderness and frugality.

So perhaps the weight of these strings of buttons is not merely physical, their patterns and structures not merely playful, their looping flexible articulation not merely sensual – although this might be sufficient.

△ **Pubic Piece. Rowena Gough.** Fine silver, sterling silver. Threaded tubular fabrication. 91 x 13 x 4 cm (36¼ x 5¼ x 1⅝ in). 1996

Channel Tryst. Rope. Rowena Gough. Antique 1920s mother-of-pearl buttons, sterling silver. Forged silver wires cross-woven to form a continuous structural linkage of 2-hole buttons. 150 x 3.5 x 1 cm (59 x 1⅜ x ⅜ in). 1997

Snake Stack. Neckpiece. Rowena Gough. Antique 1920s mother-of-pearl shell buttons, 750 gold. Forged gold wire, threaded with 2-hole buttons. 65 x 11 x 1.4 cm (26 x 4¼ x ½ in). 1996

Rachelle Thiewes' meticulous craftsmanship is expressed through perfectly repeated generic forms of tapered tubes, discs, cones and rings, through the pleasurable abundance in the stringing and bunching and, especially, through their kinetic interaction with the body. Her chromatic range is restrained but abundance, complexity and sensuality combine to challenge the component simplicity and sharp precision of the independent parts, giving her work a pervasive aesthetic and a psychological ambiguity.

Necklace. Rachelle Thiewes. Silver, slate. Hollow construction, metal fabrication, slate patterns cut using a hand engraving tool. Length 68 cm (27 in). 1995

As much as these pieces depend on the sensuality of the elements – the act of repetitive making, whilst one of the jeweller's more tiresome burdens, has also, in itself, a certain sensuality – they mainly depend on their physical interplay with the wearer. On the body, they are extravagant. They hang, swing, drape, delineate, press, touch, cluster and clink. Thiewes likes to make big jewellery, and she likes to ensure that the wearer is made more aware of her own body, both in repose and in movement.

Necklace. Rachelle Thiewes. Silver, 18 ct gold, slate. Hollow construction, metal fabrication, slate patterns are cut using a hand-engraving tool. Length 64 cm (25 in) front; 18 cm (7 in) back. 1997

SENSUALITY & IMAGE

76

*Kate Wilkinson's feather pieces
suggest a position between craft and
fashion – a position which is
interesting to many young jewellers.*

*Feathers are, of course, beautiful in
themselves and for that reason have
played an important role in the
primary body ornament of many
cultures. In the modern western world
their role has been largely secondary
to dress, which, from time to time,
they have flamboyantly accessorized.
This may explain why feathers are so
rarely used by artist jewellers: they
seem too firmly embedded in the
"primitive" on the one hand and
"fashion" on the other. So it is
difficult to be "serious" with feathers.
This is a pity. Perhaps it is hard to do
something new, but the potential is
great.*

*Wilkinson has, for some time,
concentrated her attention on
combining feathers with finely crafted
metalwork and she has produced
jewellery which can be amongst the
most stunningly dramatic or softly
seductive.*

▶ *Sophie Harley's "Seahorse"
bustier, constructed with great elan,
is unashamedly a catwalk piece,
created for effect and for the fun of it.*

*Her intention, which is not weighed
down by issues or pretensions, is to
generate a sense of opulence from the
build-up, in traditional atelier style,
of linked networks of standard
elements and repeated symbols. Her
aesthetic depends on a de-focusing
and lightening of symbolic elements,
so that they sink back to work
within the richness of the overall
scheme. Seahorses are exotic
favourites.*

Dawn Gulyas has worked from within the traditions of "alternative" – that is, non-traditional – jewellery media. She has built a great command of cast and modelled plastics, pursuing these not for their own sakes, but in service of a clearly articulated personal vocabulary of form.

Her biomorphic image-objects – full ripe forms with sometimes quirky appendages and rich colours – are both protozoal and "fruity". Yet for all their fullness, they are generally lightweight – as they must be in order to function as wearables – and have the hard, unyielding shell that the material confers. So they achieve a slightly off-balance position between natural and unnatural, worldly and unworldly: their rotund earthiness complicated by banality of material, fantasy of form and colour and, quite evidently, lovingly hand-crafted, decorated surfaces.

Her cast resin piece is, on the other hand, simply gorgeous whatever it signifies. Definitely an essay in itself.

Brooch. Dawn Gulyas. Light wood, resin, rubber, steel, white metal. Carved light wood core covered in layers of thixotropic resin, textured, dyed and sanded, smaller cast pieces attached. 5 x 16 x 4 cm (2 x 6¼ x 1½ in). 1994

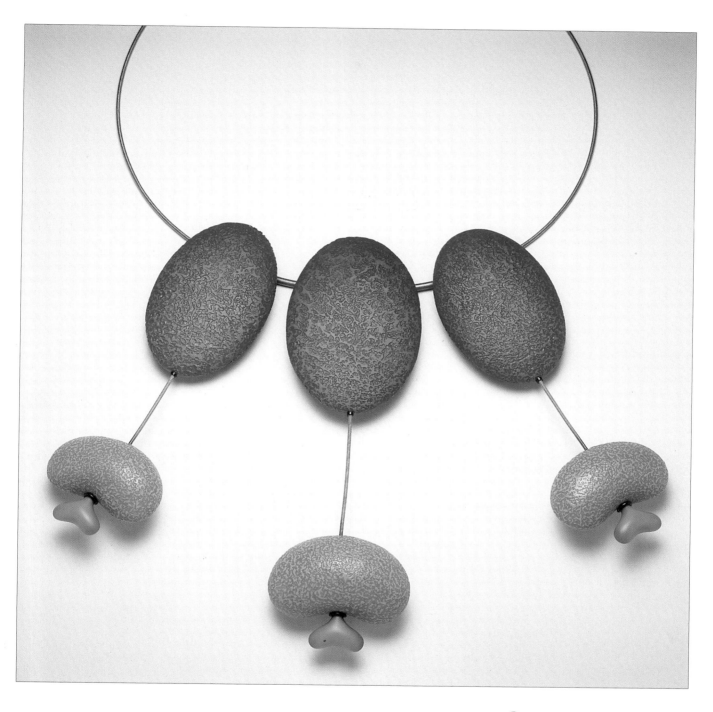

Neckpiece. Dawn Gulyas. Light wood core, resin, white metal, steel. Carved light wood core covered in layers of thixotropic resin, textured, dyed and sanded, smaller cast resin pieces attached, assembled onto steel wire. 39 x 25.5 x 3 cm (15¼ x 10 x 1¼in). 1997

 **Green with Envy.**
Elsie-Ann Hochlin.
Birch, padick.
Painted, carved wood.
30 x 40 x 40 cm
(12 x 16 x 16 in).
1997

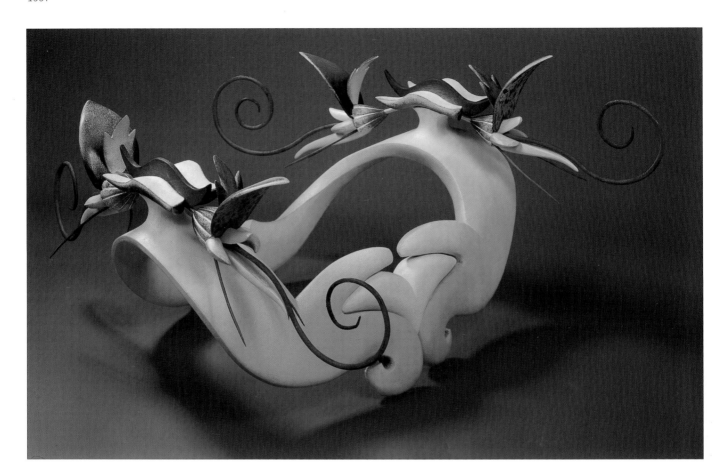

 **My Thai Cook.**
Elsie-Ann Hochlin.
Beech, birch. Painted,
carved wood.
30 x 40 x 30 cm
(12 x 16 x 12 in).
1998

 **Looking Askance.**
Elsie-Ann Hochlin.
Birch, beech, padick.
Painted, carved wood.
20 x 70 x 25 cm
(8 x 28 x 10 in). 1994

The jewellery of Elsie-Ann Hochlin is unashamedly sculptural and theatrical. It is big, boldly formed and intensely, unnaturally, colourful. The effect, "in the flesh" – they may be made of wood, but they are also in some way fleshy, like genetically-engineered succulents – is overwhelming. The sense of menace, of decadence is often inescapable. And yet these works are also persuasively beautiful to wear.

Hochlin has been daring. She has taken on what can be, for the jeweller, a seductive but dangerously banal form – the flower motif – and has given it an extraordinarily expressive and innovative twist. She has also, in her carved pieces, perhaps with as much joy and reverence as daring, taken on a traditional decorative craft, a form which can so easily lapse into vacuousness – and has pumped it full of hormones.

No doubt these pieces can be used in their own right as decorative objects, but their intention and their real power can only be appreciated when they are thrust into relationship with the body – a stunning and surreal aggregation.

Strange Flower. Elsie-Ann Hochlin. Birch, beech. Painted, carved wood. 40 x 60 x 40 cm (16 x 24 x 16 in). 1994

81

Queen Bee's Sting. Elsie-Ann Hochlin. Birch, padick, plastic padding. Painted, carved wood. 25 x 40 x 30 cm (10 x 16 x 12 in). 1994

The jewellery of Miranda
Watkins emerges from
within craft traditions
but is headed firmly in
the direction of style and
fashion.

She combines a
deliberately restrained
and direct simplicity in
the handling of
materials with severe
geometry in overall form.
Her approach as a maker
is in some respects
diffident, so that the
objects can speak more
plainly for the wearer
and the ensemble, but
she is unafraid of bold
statements in style.

Her constructions are
based on tension systems
– assembly without
solder or adhesive. Her
working method and
aesthetic is to articulate
the essential qualities of
metal, restricting its
expression through
surface and edge, line
and junction. The results
make big gestures in
shape, light and
movement. These pieces
are evidently destined for
the catwalk and the
street.

Neckpiece, Earrings and Bracelet. Miranda Watkins. Crystal, stainless steel, perspex. Tension held constructions. Neckpiece: 90 cm (35½ in); earrings: 9.5 x 6.5 cm (3¾ x 2½ in); bracelet: 12 x 12 cm (4¾ x 4¾ in). 1993

Bags, Earrings. Miranda Watkins. Stainless steel, aluminium and perspex. Stainless steel mesh formed under pressure and bolted into frames. Bags, left to right: approx. 30 x 23 cm (12 x 9 in); 15 x 28 cm (6 x 11 in); 47 x 38 cm (18½ x 15 in); earrings: 6.5 x 6.5 cm (2½ x 2½ in). 1993

Bracelet. Miranda Watkins. Anodized aluminium, stainless steel. Tension held construction. 23.5 x 23.5 x 4 cm (9¼ x 9¼ x 1½ in). 1990

SENSUALITY & IMAGE

Naomi Filmer's jewellery explores places where jewellery rarely goes – the soft spaces between fingers and toes, inside the mouth, around the intimate contours of the ear.

She will use simple constructions to open mouths, and even LED's to light up the resultant orifice, but her typical forms, although of metal, are exceptionally organic. They have a surreal, biomorphic character which arises in part from the classic jewellery technique of wax modelling and casting. In her pieces, however, the manipulation of warm, soft wax creates small forms which sneak around, between and into the body.

Filmer's works are occasionally demonstrative but more usually locked into intimate sensations, not only through perception of image but also through actual experience of sensuality. A strong sense of intimacy between object and body is essential and inescapable: these pieces make little or no sense out of context. This is their meaning.

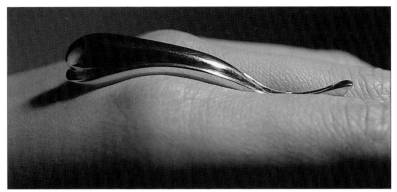

Finger Between. Naomi Filmer. Silver. Lost wax casting. 6 x 3.6 x 1.2 cm (2¼ x 1½ x ½ in). 1993

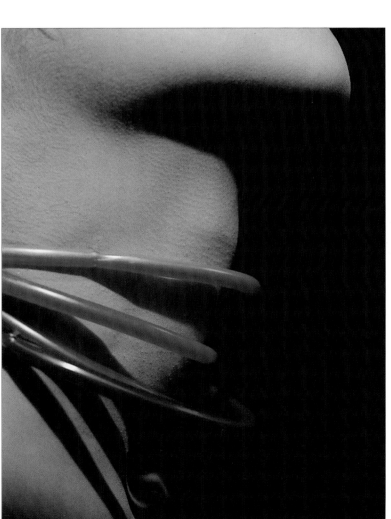

Rubber Chokers. Naomi Filmer. UV tubing, silver. Fabrication. Tubing 0.6 x 12 cm (¼ x 4¾ in). 1996/1998

● **Ear-Under. Naomi Filmer.** Silver. Lost wax casting and fabrication (soldered, formed). Approx. 2.5 x 3 x 0.8 cm (1 x 1¼ x ⅜ in). 1998

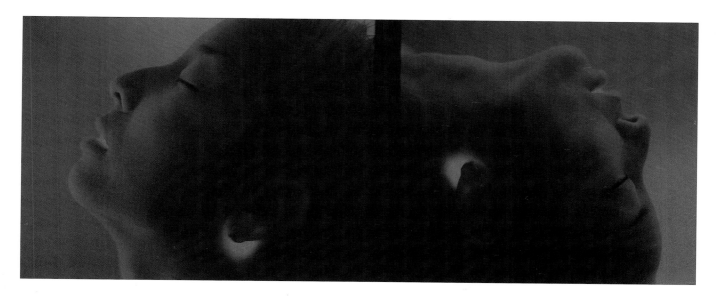

△ **Mouthlight and Earlight. Naomi Filmer.** Resin, LEDs and battery. Cast resin and hand work. 3.8 x 1.5 x 1.3 cm (1½ x ⅝ x ½ in) and 1.6 x 1.5 cm (¾ x ⅝ in). 1995

The design partners of Articular have made a series of jewels formed from casts of human vertebrae.

Their strategy, of exteriorizing internal elements of the body so that they become its ornament, is not uncommon in contemporary architecture but is unusual in jewellery. The antecedents for this type of jewellery can of course be traced to the wearing of animal bones both for ornament and for their magical properties.

Articular state, "we were interested in examining the 'female muse', the fashion objectification of womanhood, especially in relation to taboos". In common with a number of contemporary designers whose work is focused through a fashion context, they are aware that their intellectual resolution is framed, sometimes paradoxically, by feminist critique. Their final expression, however, with its overtones of animism and even cannibalism, conveys a dark and sensual complexity.

◯ **Backpiece. Articular.** White pewter and buffalo leather. Cast from a human backbone, modelled and re-cast to form interlinked back lace fastened onto leather. 75 cm (30 in) long. 1996

◯ **Handpiece. Articular.** Stirling silver. Modelled from wax cast of human spine. 7.5 x 5 x 15 cm (3 x 2 x 6 in). 1997

Typical of the work of Karl Fritsch is its sculptural quality and its wide range of designs which span from archaic to post-modern styles. He also has a vision which is unerringly, mischievously erotic. Even when this is not overt, it is nevertheless present in the morphologies he explores with such rapt attention.

In a positive sense his artistic creations are coincidental, as he develops his pieces during the working process. However, nothing is left to chance. His choice and application of stones are unconventional and his use of metals uninhibited by value. Silver or gold is cast in free-modelled forms and left in an unpolished state. Thus, the jewellery takes on a primitive air, and is reminiscent of prehistoric finds. Even broken jewellery parts are cannibalized to simultaneously retain the original character and create a new image.

Fritsch questions on many levels the nature of jewellery and the role it plays in our lives.

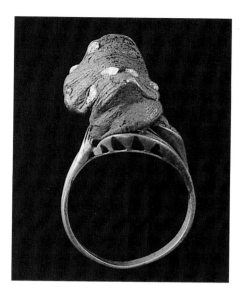

Ring. Karl Fritsch. Silver, white gold 585, cubic zirkonia. Cast on built ring. Ring size 56. 1995

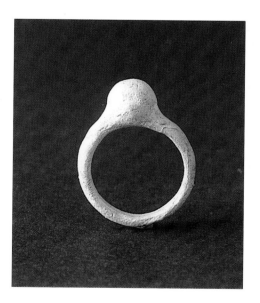

Ring. Karl Fritsch. Silver. Modelled and cast. Ring size 56. 1994

Brooch. Karl Fritsch. Copper, coated tin, palladium silver, amethyst. Repoussé, constructed. 10 x 8 x 3 cm (4 x 3⅛ x 1¼ in). 1992

Theo Smeets makes jewels which have an almost visceral sensuality and are overlaid with a tangible aura of intimacy. Within this genre of form, feeling and expression they are outstanding examples.

The necklace, with its pearl droplets and primitive yet delicate wire technique, carrying forever the memory of the touch of its maker's hands and yet signifying another bond for its wearer, lays on the skin, darkly ravishing, proudly worn. The pendants, less subtle perhaps – one pair with magnetic attraction – hint at a more open and explicit declaration of the realm of the senses.

Anouk. Theo Smeets.
Sterling silver, gold 585, feathers, magnets. Fabricated. Length 10 cm (4 in). 1996

 **Home, Sweet Home. Theo Smeets.** Sterling silver, acrylic, nylon, magnet. Fabricated. 8 cm (1¼ in). 1996

De Zwarte Weduwe (The Black Widow). Theo Smeets. Sterling silver, rose quartz, magnets. Fabricated. Length 60 cm (23½ in). 1996

**Necklace.
Dorothy Hogg.** Silver and gold. Formed, soldered, etched. Length 50 cm (20 in). 1994

Dorothy Hogg's design and working methods revolve around purity of form, movement, sound and interaction with the body.

Her vision depends on a reductive process, affecting line, form, surface and juncture. All are articulated with an objective eye, which focuses on clarity. She finds endlessly interesting the permutations and repetitions of the pod-like forms which have become her signature. Their constrained volumes and sharp points imply mildly charged tensions at work within compositional schemes which are otherwise carefully modest.

In the end, loose movement and the light clash of parts is perhaps Hogg's guiding aesthetic impulse, but underlying ambiguities seem also to play a subtle role in our perception of the objects in relation to the body.

91

Jacky Oliver has found a new point of departure for constructions on the body. She has begun from observations of muscle stretching and relaxing excercises, and has "extrapolated" depictions of the forces at work. The results, although based on close and selective observation, are intuitive and metaphorical rather than scientific and analytical.

Oliver's piece quite clearly "belongs" to the body as it assumes a certain attitude, and the two are inseparable components of a single composition. In a very limited sense this is perhaps not jewellery, but in the sense that it is constructed for the body and ornaments the expression of physicality, it certainly occupies the territory of jewellery.

Here is another artist worrying at the conflict between generalized jewellery artefacts and jewellery which beyond doubt must connect to an individual human being. Unusually, if not uniquely, her route is physical rather than psychological.

THEMES & NARRATIVES

FOR ARTISTS WHO WISH TO EXPLORE the world of ideas and experience, whether cultural, political, sociological or personal, jewellery can be a special but appropriate vehicle. The language employed may be either literal or metaphorical. Ideas are transformed into objects. This is especially effective where these ideas intersect with the traditional forms and meanings of jewellery, which becomes a testing ground for questions, provocations, emotions and allegory. The capacity of individual pieces to sustain a greater breadth of content, within the boundaries of the uses of jewellery, is increasingly under trial.

Figure Pin No. 140. Bruce Metcalf. Maple, copper, brass, 14 ct gold, 23 ct gold leaf. Carved, electroformed. 4¾ x 2¾ in (56 x 77 cm). 1997

Lost and Found. Lin Cheung. Silver, fine gold. Neckhoop: cast and planished. Ø 30cm (12in); ring is life size. 1997

Emotional Repair (Travel Size). Lin Cheung. Silver, paper, acetate, stainless steel, gold-plated silver wire, darning needle. Folded silver sheet. 5 x 5 cm (2 x 2 in). 1998

Worth (My Weight in Gold). Lin Cheung. Silver, gold plate, stainless steel. Hollow construction, struck details. Pendant: 5 x 2.5 cm (2 x 1 in); neckpiece Ø 12 cm (4¾ in). 1998

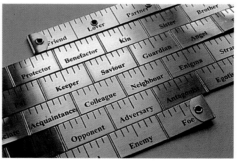

Friend or Foe (detail). Lin Cheung. Silver, 18 ct gold. Photo-etched silver. 150 cm (59 in) long. 1998

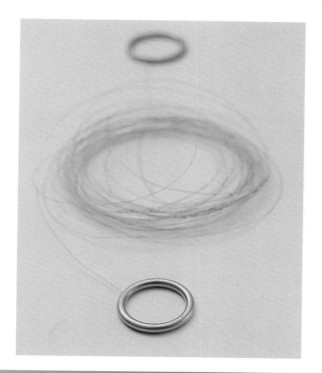

◁▷ ◁▽ **How Long is a Piece of String? Lin Cheung.** Silver, gold plate. Connected rings. Life-size rings and approx. 600 cm (236 in) of wire. 1997

With a quotation from St. Bede, Lin Cheung offers a poetic insight on the feelings that contextualize her work:

"As if when on a winter's night you sit feasting with your ealdormen and thegns, a single sparrow should fly swiftly into the hall, and in coming in at one door instantly fly out through another. In that time in which it is indoors it is indeed not touched by the fury of the winter, but

yet, this smallest space of calmness being passed almost in a flash, from winter going into winter again, it is lost to your eyes."

Cheung's spare, witty, sometimes wry, but finely honed and essentially modern or post-modern forms are only tangentially linked with received perceptions of the early mediaeval court. Their purpose, of course, is not to mark points in time, but to fix feelings, brief insights which are in

their way timeless or – like the sparrow – "in the air". With refreshing and honest simplicity, but also with the knowing guile of a skilful goldsmith, she explores the capacity of jewellery at once to express and to objectify truths about relationships.

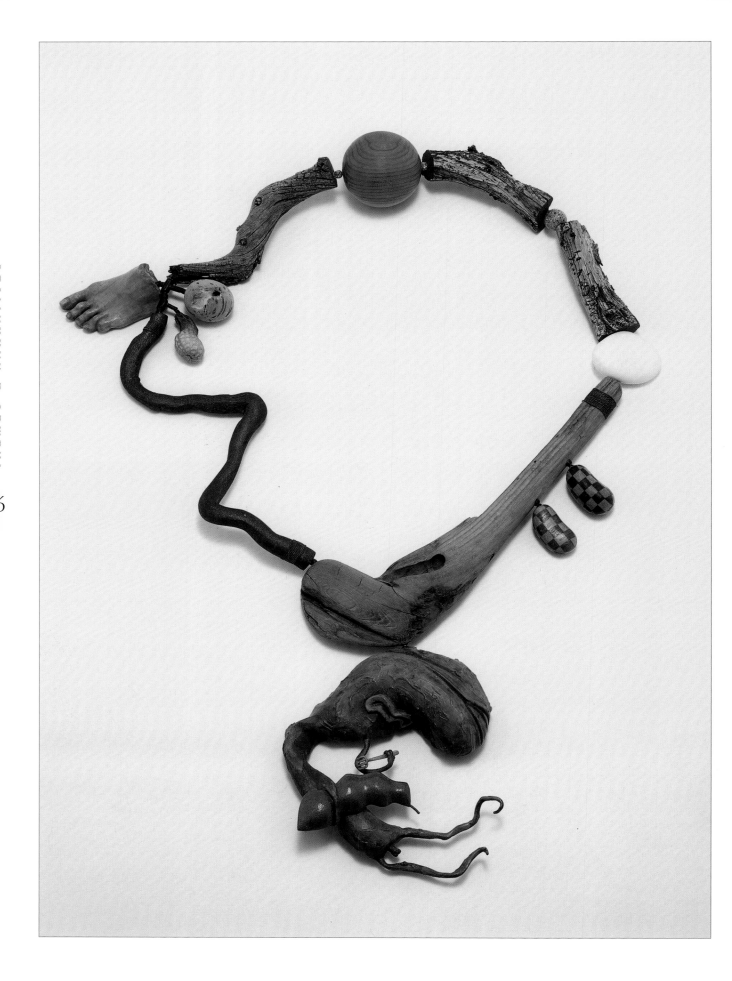

For Bruce Metcalf, jewellery offers a direct and unfettered means of communication – a special luxury in a discipline, the very art of which is characteristically to conceal, disguise or otherwise harness and suppress its underlying impulses.

⬤ **Wood Necklace No. 12. Bruce Metcalf.** Various woods, cork, brass, sterling silver, aluminium, copper, stainless steel cable, Corian® , peanut, urethane resin. Painted, carved, cast, fabricated. 40.6 x 33cm (16 x 13 in). 1994

⬤ **Figure Pin No. 147. Bruce Metcalf.** Maple, copper, brass, silver, acrylic plastic, Delrin® , 23k gold leaf. Carved, electroformed, fabricated. 12.7 x 8.9 cm and 3.8 x 2.5 cm (5 x 3½ and 1½ x 1 in). 1997

Metcalf combines elements of self perception with a kind of free association, in a way which leads to some of the most arresting images in the contemporary canon. They certainly test our sense of what is appropriate in ornament – it seems redundant to point out that they do not conform to "normal" perceptions of jewellery, from which they are about as far removed as it is possible to imagine – but they carry an aura of honesty and authenticity which cannot be dismissed.

The results are often outrageous: amusing and disturbing by turns. And if one accepts that jewellery should, in the first place, be a vehicle for the expression of the artist, then they clearly carry that idea to a logical extreme, and beyond – making a direct appeal to one's sense of the human condition. From that standpoint, they can be worn as signs of complicity as much as from any desire to shock or entertain.

Pierre Degen, a skilful and classically trained goldsmith, is best known for his large sculptural or performance pieces, objects which test perceptions and limits of jewellery and wearability.

In contrast are his pieces made of tin cans and rubber inner tubes from bicycles. Here he has been more pragmatic and differently ideological.

Degen's encounters with the homeless in the Charing Cross area of London gave him cause for reflection on the affordability of jewellery and why the poor should be deprived of something decorative to wear. As tinned food is a basic nutrition available to the homeless, he had the idea of recycling the tin cans, polishing them, and, in combination with other re-used materials, designing appealing jewellery for the deprived. In total effect, however, things are rarely so simple. It is impossible to escape the sense that these are also art objects, reflecting as they do a recognition and appropriation of Duchampian strategies.

Possibly more unconsciously and prosaically, Degen's jewellery meets the ecological concerns of our times by using recycled materials.

▼ **Bracelet. Pierre Degen.** Tin can, rubber flooring, carpet underlay, inner tube. Assembled (The elastic, cut from inner tube, is holding everything together.) Ø 8.5 cm (3¼ in), length 11 cm (4¼ in). 1995

◤ **Pendant. Pierre Degen.** Tin can, wood, nail, inner tube. Nailed and knotted. 26 x 12.5 x 8 cm (10¼ x 5 x 3¼ in). 1995

Margrit Linder shows a selection from "Fingerbags", a project which gently questions definitions of jewellery whilst encouraging participation and exchange.

Taking as a starting point some small plastic bags with finger holes designed for carrying found objects, she advanced the concept that these amounted to finger rings or sculptures for the hand. They offered a unifying form which would be the basis for audience participation in an exhibition. Inventive solutions would multiply, and the exhibition grow, according to the number of active responses. Participants would also have a chance to win, by lottery, examples submitted by the artist or others.

This idea may be fun, but it also cleverly exploits a whole range of dynamics in jewellery, exhibited art, social behaviour, politics. Its tacit theme, however, is to expose the intuition that owners of jewellery somehow form a hidden membership or network within society, that they are associated by their appreciation of, and complicity in, its values.

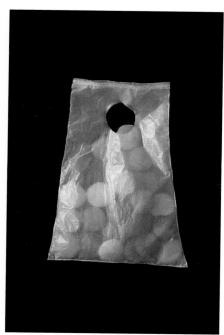

🔺 **Fingerbags. Margrit Linder.** Plastic. Empty fingerbags sent with an invitation to participants to fill with chosen materials. These are some of the returned bags. 11 x 7.5 cm (4½ x 3 in). 1997

Laliquiana # 1. Susan Cohn. Oakley red iridium, plutonite sunglass lenses, Sony wind socks, orange, olive green, emerald green, olive brown aluminium, 375 pink gold, stainless steel cable, condom. Hand-constructed. Insect 15 x 14 cm (6 x 5½ in). 1995

Installation of Catch Me. Susan Cohn. 30,000 bolt rings in 925 silver, rolled gold, 375 gold, aluminium plate. Assembled. 1998

Susan Cohn works within a range of conceptual frames, from stylish industrial production objects to gallery installation art. Her current jewellery is a vehicle for commentary on contemporary life – and jewellery itself – with undertones of ecological concerns.

She focuses on the assemblage, recycling and transformation of what can be appropriated from the obsolescent waste of the street into fantastic wearables. The result is anti-craft, anti-art; a celebration of the provisional; intentionally banal and superficial, but also somehow angst-ridden, images of a litter-bin, street-style aesthetic: one which would "party on" through the last days of an imploding industrial culture.

Cohn's use of discarded sunglasses and aerials is telling of noise and glitter in the darkness. Hers is in some ways a dark vision, and her own antennae are twitching nervously.

◇ **Reflections. Susan Cohn.** Photograph: Cibachrome
print; insect: Oakley red iridium Plutonite sunglass
lenses, Sony wind socks, orange, olive green, emerald
green, olive brown anodized aluminium, 375 pink gold,
stainless steel cable, condom. Assembled.
Insect: 15 x 14 cm (6 x 5½ in). 1995

Brune Boyer-Pellerej has shown a consistent fascination for North African architecture and its exotic interiors. One of its most important features was the moucharabie – the harem door, made of finely pierced wood, to protect the ladies from forbidden viewers. This group of brooches was inspired by a stay in Spain, a country which for centuries was under Arab rule and where its influence on the arts is still evident.

She has been inspired not only by the decorative effects of wood carvings, but also by the play of light and shadow through intricate openings.

This effect appears to be remembered in the brooches. Their latticework of gold or silver articulates tiny exterior openings and grander interior ornament. This play on inside and outside contributes to the romance, the mystery and the cultural readings of her jewellery.

△ **Château en Espagne - Pin. Brune Boyer-Pellerej.** Wenge wood, gold. Carved and woven. 3 x 10 cm (1¼ x 4 in). 1994

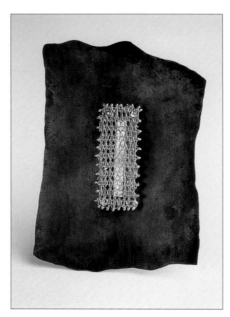

△ **Château en Espagne - Pin (back). Brune Boyer-Pellerej.** Steel, gold, silver. Hammered and woven. 7 x 9 cm (2¾ x 3½ in). 1995

△ **Château en Espagne - Pin (front). Brune Boyer-Pellerej.** Steel, gold, silver. Hammered and woven. 7 x 9 cm (2¾ x 3½ in). 1995

Anette Wohlleber deals in dreams and memories but indirectly by association rather than by linear narrative.

Her work is in some respects haptic – to be understood by touch – in that surfaces, edges are busy, worn, eroded. But all of this can in fact be taken in by the eyes. It is not subtle, but emphatic. The sense of erosion, in particular, works on the imagination as does a fossil – half seen, half understood.

She squarely addresses the world of the imagination. Her works must be interpreted from the experience of a fairy-tale landscape. They do, however, stand somewhat apart from sentimentality by reason of their surreal physicality – an adult interpretation. Our responses remain uncertain, personal and sometimes inexpressible, but she is sure in touching the child within us.

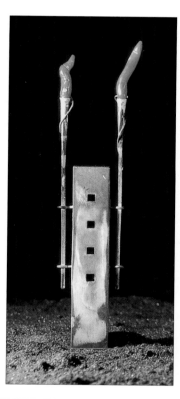

Verbrannte Erde (Burnt Soil) (brooch). Anette Wohlleber. Silver, gold, corals. Forged, soldered, assembled. Approx. 10 x 3 x 1.5 cm (4 x 1¼ x ⅝ in). 1996

Frau Holle (brooch). Anette Wohlleber. Silver, gold, citrin. Forged, soldered and assembled, set stone. 10 x 8.5 x 2.5 cm (4 x 3⅜ x 1 in). 1996

Seeräuberschiff (Pirate Ship) (brooch). Anette Wohlleber. Silver, enamel, found glass stone, sapphire. Cast, sawn, soldered, assembled, set stones, enamelled. 11 x 6 x 1.5 cm (4¾ x 2¼ x ⅝ in). 1994/95

Kadri Mälk's theme is "human vulnerability and the shadow theatre of life".

Jewellery is an art of small objects, and not very tolerant of broad themes. It easily becomes overloaded, the object collapsing, disintegrating under the weight of meaning attached to it. But Mälk succeeds in presenting complex autobiographical intuitions within condensed poetic narratives.

Her objects are made up of fragments, brought together but remaining disquietingly apart: experiences which connect only obliquely or momentarily in the imagination. Her selections from the chaos of life, in the form of amulets, offer bridges of meaning between experience and memory, between the mind and the senses. Crucially, everything is "fixed" by the many gestures of making, in the same way that a complex composition in painting can be held together by the handling of paint on a surface.

The objects offer intimations of shared experience. They frame private worlds within a capricious external world.

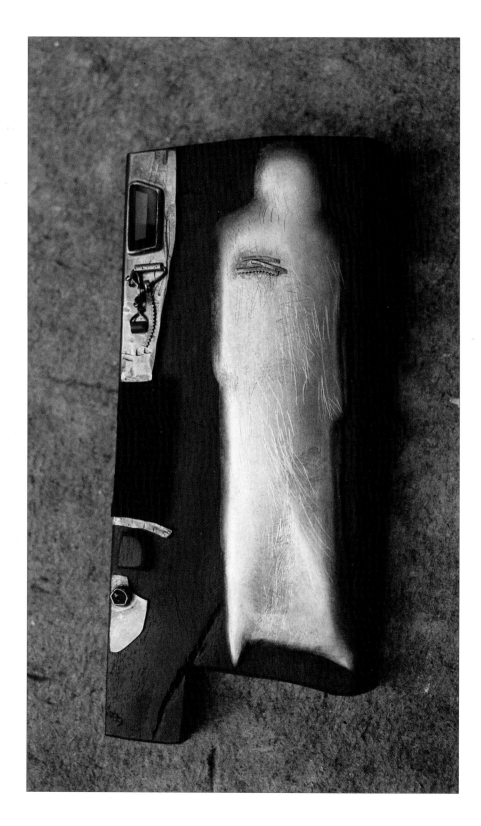

▶ **Sad angel (brooch). Kadri Mälk.** Silver, ebony, tourmaline-indigolite, rubber, malachite, spinel. Repoussé, cut stone, carved wood. Length 7 cm (2¾ in). 1995

Résistance III Olivia (sacrifice plate) Kadri Mälk. Wood, rubber, iron, silver, gold, photo, moleskin, black coral, smoky quartz, olivine. Carved wood, painting, cut stone. 14 x 12.5 cm (5½ x 5 in). 1997

Résistance I Anna (sacrifice plate). Kadri Mälk. Wood, rubber, silver, slate, wax, iron, black coral, shark's tooth, cordierite. Cut stone, carved wood, painting, repoussé. 10.5 x 14.5 cm (4¼ x 5¾ in). 1997

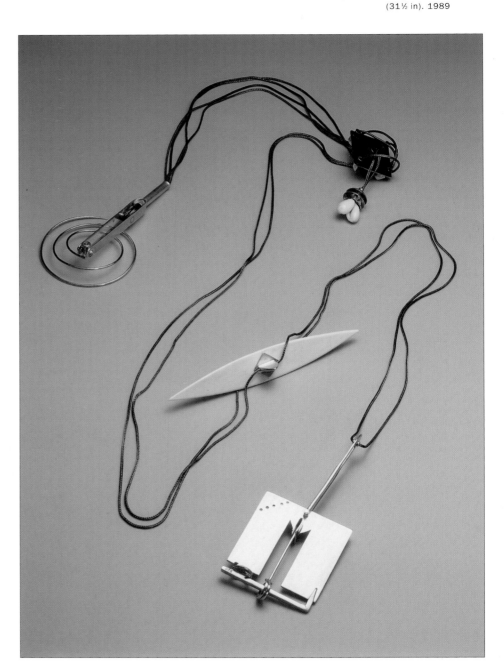

⬙ **Body Piece.**
Deganit Schocken.
Silver, steel,
plastic, shells.
Mixed techniques.
Length 80 cm
(31½ in). 1989

Modesty, finesse and smallness of scale are words which best describe the jewellery of Deganit Schocken.

Her concept of a chain is unconventional, the disconnected jewellery ornaments, mainly oxidized white silver, become a scattered composition against the garment or body. The simplicity of the spiral, a fundamental shape in design, preoccupies her in particular. Further recurring elements in her work are the propellor shape, as sculptural form in motion, and the building-like pendant, as architectural structure. She makes "stones" and ornaments out of available materials, either from nature, as in the chain, or, in the case of the brooches, uses a pattern of sewing threads and earring fittings.

Schocken's reflections on space, environment and the human landscape are most evident in the aerial-view brooches. These are conceived as a ground plan with miniature features – signs of habitation, existence, memory and myth – their evocation achieved by direct and almost innocent fabrication. They are challengingly simple but deft transformations.

◉ **Two Brooches.**
Deganit Schocken.
Silver, gold, cotton
thread, semi-precious
stones, readymade
gold earring fasteners.
Mixed techniques.
11 x 4.5 cm
(4¼ x 1¾ in) each.
1997

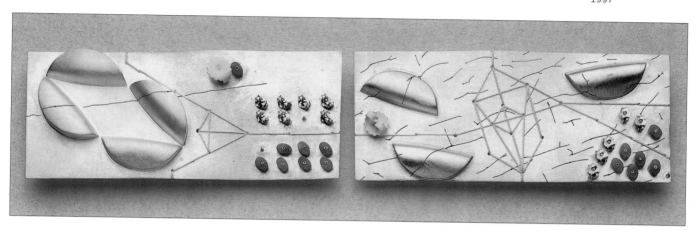

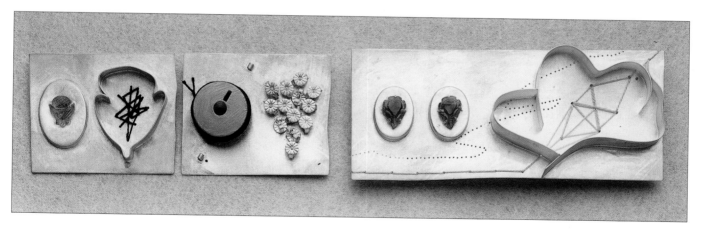

◬ **Three Brooches.**
Deganit Schocken.
Silver, cotton threads,
semi precious stones,
readymade sewing
machine bobbin and
silver earring
fasteners. Mixed
techniques.
5 x 4.5 cm (2 x 1¾ in)
and 11 x 4.5 cm
(4¼ x 1¾ in). 1997

Amanda Mansell describes her pieces as "symbolic, honest and sometimes aggressive theatrical statements that deal with the beauty façade and the hidden horrors of pain and discomfort". She is not alone in utilizing jewellery to explore wider issues of cultural pressures endured by women, particularly those of ideal beauty, but she has done so with an open gestural quality which is at once set apart from, and engaged with, images of style and fashion.

Incidents within the pieces themselves provide rich pickings for the imagination. Pearls – symbols of beauty but also redolent of the banal strung accessory – are here contained by, trapped in, glass... which is "pure" but brittle. Their careful cohesion is easily broken. They segue into a chain which is gilded. At first this seems appropriate for a necklace but it is too heavy for such a purpose, and soon becomes a dead weight – a burden, a symbol of willing or unwilling enslavement. This piece alone amounts to an outstanding statement.

Mansell has nevertheless shown with disarming simplicity and delicious wit that jewellery can be made to be both polemical and modish. And the truth of this is demonstrated by the readiness with which her work is taken up for iconic treatment by a fashion magazine – a many-layered cultural feedback.

Neckpiece. Amanda Mansell. Rope, stainless steel, brass, gold plate. Fabricated, turned. Length 300 cm (118 in). 1997

Neckpiece. Amanda Mansell. Rope, silver. Fabricated. Length 200 cm (79 in). 1997

Follow My Lead. Amanda Mansell. Silver, mild steel, pearls. Fabricated, forged. Length 200 cm (79 in). 1997

Nicole Gratiot Stöber's startling concept was that a piece of jewellery might function as the signal and witness of a physical relationship – the literal transformation of an emotional charge into a thing of light and electrical energy.

These objects are from Stöber's first student experiments. They are brought to life by touch – in itself an eloquent metaphor for the relationship of the jewel to the living body – but that is not all.
Two matching rings are ignited only when their wearers clasp hands. A wand-like object, as it passes from one person to another, narrates moments of meeting and sharing in a translation of energy. In these examples, the underlying concept is emphasized and exposed by their simplicity and minimalism of form.

The neckpiece implies more complex thematic developments. Seen across a room, approached, and touched on its invitingly thorny points, it registers this contact by setting off a running string of red LEDs around the wearer's neck – a rush of excitement which is disturbingly entangled with symbolism and irony.

Neckpiece. **Nicole Gratiot Stöber.** Gold, perspex, touch sensitive microelectronics with LED. Cast, machined plastic and metal, custom electronics. 1994

**Light Brooches.
Nicole Gratiot Stöber.**
Stainless steel,
perspex, magnets,
touch sensitive
microelectronics with
LED. Machined plastic
and metal, custom
electronics. 1994

**Light Brooch. Nicole
Gratiot Stöber.** Stainless
steel, perspex, magnets,
touch sensitive
microelectronics with
LED. Machined plastic
and metal, custom
electronics. 1994

**For Two Rings.
Nicole Gratiot Stöber.**
Gold, silver, perspex,
magnet, touch
sensitive
microelectronics with
LED. Machined plastic
and metal, custom
electronics. 1994

Love is Like a Butterfly (detail). Mah Rana. Second-hand gold wedding rings, butterflies. Fabricated. Overall wall installation: 90 x 90 cm (35½ x 35½ in). 1998

His 'n' Hers. Mah Rana. Two second-hand gold wedding rings, one left untouched, the other reworked into wire to create a new ring with cage. Height 6.5 cm (2½ in). 1996

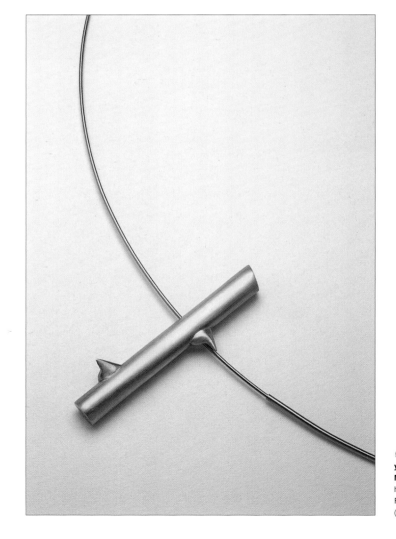

I Never Promised you a Rose Garden. Mah Rana. Second-hand wedding ring. Fabricated. 45 cm (17¾ in) high. 1996

◄ *Mah Rana comments on relationships from the understanding of both jeweller and woman.*

Rana's stance is at the same time matter-of-fact and ironic. She embraces the jeweller's role in cementing relationships, but with wry observation and delicious mischief.

She has taken the concept that gold wedding rings, although shaped and given to symbolize a unique eternal bond, are often, in the way of the world, finally melted down to reemerge in another, perhaps similar guise. She has followed this logic through by fabricating new rings from reclaimed old rings. She is herself caught in, but enjoying, a kind of trap, a loop. She is a willing maker of rings, but is compelled to comment on the bondage they may represent.

Out of this sense of uneasy complicity, Rana has come up with some objects which are startling but beautifully understated: they are subdued and dignified by a maker's care, respect and restraint. The image of real butterflies set upon or escaping from symbolically binding gold rings will sit in the mind for a very long time.

⬡ **Golden Locks II.**
Adele Tipler. Copper, gold lacquer. Electroformed.
35 x 20 x 20cm (15¾ x 8 x 8 in).
1996

Adele Tipler's bold, gestural headpieces have made a genuinely original and liberating contribution to the field of electroformed jewellery.

Tipler's baroque vision is allowed full play by the electroforming process and her imagery is often at its strongest when it seems, coincidentally, to refer to the underwater creatures or accretions of nature. This is not, however, the only resonance. Her thematic developments have led to a reinterpretation of the most striking and expressively mannered historic and cultural forms of headwear, translating structures of textile and hair into lightweight metal.

△ **Golden Bun.**
Adele Tipler. Copper, gold lacquer. Electroformed.
40 x 20 x 20cm (16 x 8 x 8 in). 1996

THEMES & NARRATIVES

Ted Noten has followed the logic of a simple process – casting found objects into synthetic resin and literally incorporating them into jewellery. There the logic and simplicity ends, however, because they also become objects which tease the imagination and turn in on the profession of jewellery itself.

In jewellery history terms, they refer to amber: the natural resin which, oozing from trees, can trap and embed insects, fixing them for all time, and which has for centuries been prized as an alternative to precious stones. So these pieces continue a tradition.

But Noten's purpose is not simply to fix objects which will make "pretty" jewellery any more than it is to simply shock. His humour and mischief is thoughtfully directed. The mouse, found dead, has been given a pearl necklace and set within a neckpiece. So honoured, as in an amulet or reliquary, it has escaped anonymity, becoming a "princess" amongst mice, but also carrying all the irony which artist jewellers reserve for the ubiquitous string of pearls. The gold plated transistor chip is similarly elevated,

appropriated and revered for its jewel-like and artful miniature precision. On another tack, a "heart" is pumped up by touching a ring – a conflation of symbols.

▽ **Ring. Ted Noten.**
Silver, polyurethane.
(Air pump blows air into heart to inflate it.)
8 cm (3¼ in). 1997

△ **Chip-Ring. Ted Noten.** Transistor chip, gold, resin, Cast.
4 x 2.7 x 1.2 cm
(1½ x 1 x ½ in). 1996

△ **Princess (pendant). Ted Noten.** Mouse, pearl chain, acrylic, silver, steel string. Cast.
16 x 7.5 x 4 cm
(6¼ x 3 x 1½ in).
1995

▽ You Know...My Flower...I Am Responsible For Her (separated). Claudia Langer.

▽ You Know...My Flower...I Am Responsible For Her (together). Claudia Langer. Sterling silver, glass, rose. Soldered. 1.3 x 1.7 x 7.8 mm (½ x ¾ x 3 in). 1997

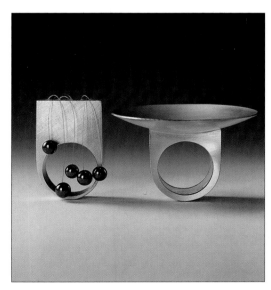

⬠ Mother and Daughter (separated). Claudia Langer.

⬠ Mother and Daughter (together). Claudia Langer. Sterling silver, hematite, nylon. Soldered. 4.7 x 4.7 x 3.4 cm (1¾ x 1¾ x 1½ in). 1997

Claudia Langer is not presently alone in directly addressing human relationships through and within the forms of jewellery. Her motif of interlocking rings recurs throughout the ages as a symbol of kinship or love, but she is exploring her own territory within the genre.

Concepts of giving and sharing, signals and secrets are implicitly at or near the heart of jewellery. Langer is intent upon developing these concepts as thematic material through explicit and metaphorical narratives. So the rings which are two are also one, and the symbolic rose-ring which can be removed and given as a token of love nevertheless in some way needs the protective dome-ring. Whilst the two have meanings when apart, they are most fulfilled when together.

In such ways, her reflections on the nature of relationships, which might of course be symbolized by a ring, are given symbolic form within the actual ring that is made. The process, one may say, is one of giving literal form to the abstractions of attractions. It's a demanding theme, dependent in practice on the resolution of tricky formal and constructional problems, but it's a good one – and one with mileage in it.

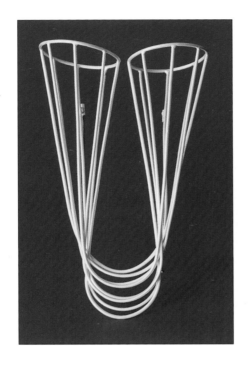

⬙ **Untitled (from the series E-Motion). Xavier Domènech.** Silver. Metalwork. 6.7 x 6.5 x 3.7 cm (2¾ x 2½ x 1½ in). 1998

◗ **Untitled (from the series E-Motion). Xavier Domènech.** Silver. Metalwork. 9 x 5.5 x 2.6 cm (3½ x 2¼ x 1 in). (3½ x 2¼ x 1 in). 1998

116

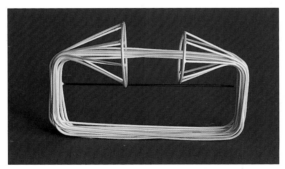

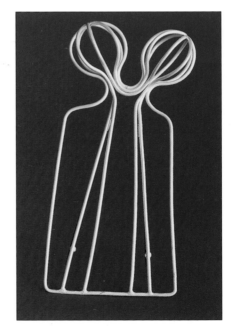

△ **Untitled (from the series E-Motion). Xavier Domènech.** Silver. Metalwork. 8 x 5.2 x 2.7 cm (3¼ x 2⅛ x 1¼. 1998

◖ **Untitled (from the series E-Motion). Xavier Domènech.** Silver. Metalwork. 9.1 x 4.2 x 2 cm (3½ x 1½ x ¾ in). 1998

Xavier Domènech has been described as a poet and philosopher who makes jewellery which revolves around the existence of the immortal soul.

For him, the body is the temple of the soul. The jewel should therefore be the icon, the idol, the symbol. Symbols live within us, and our world is full of symbols – as shown in his amuletic rings from the series "Esclava" (Slaves). The ring, traditionally understood as a form without beginning or end, has been interpreted as a sign of bondage, confirmed here by the anchor, shackle and toggle on the bezels.

Slaves (Rings to Femme Fatale) left to right: Eva, Medusa, The Sirens, Maria Magdalena. Xavier Domènech. Gold, silver. Metalwork. Ring sizes: Eva, 19; Medusa, 12; The Sirens, 15; Maria Magdalena, 15. 1996/7

Dynamic silver wire structures form a series of brooches titled "E-Motion" (Energy on/in Motion). The animated outlines of the wires define interleaving, interpenetrating volumes or receptacles in spatial terms, their psychological content resulting in a virtual conversation between the jewellery, wearer and viewer.

Domènech's decorative pieces are full of personal ideas and conceal complex, sometimes secret messages or mysteries, but first they have presence.

Philip Sajet is amongst the most inventive and individualistic of contemporary jewellers, his interest flitting openly from the common-place to the exotic, as if browsing in a catalogue of possibilities.

If no subject matter may not be grist for Sajet's mill, nor does he employ any fixed style, preferring to be free of such conditions. His work, however, always seems to combine a certain unmodern delicacy and traditional pragmatism with a more contemporary edginess. He takes a direct approach to the composition and amalgamation of elements – a kind of undesignerly design – expressing impatience with craftiness and preciousness. Deploying such strategies, he keeps both the content and the making superficially fresh and unmediated, whilst also indelibly imprinting them with his own attitudes.

All in all, it is difficult to pin down, this blend of matter-of-fact attitude with sophisticated insider intelligence.

◊ **Ring.**
Philip Sajet. Diamonds, rock crystal, glue. Fabricated, assembled. Height 21 mm (⅚ in). 1995

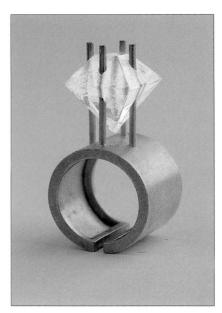

◊ **Parasite Ring.**
Philip Sajet. Gold, rock crystal. Fabricated, assembled. Height approx. 5 cm (2 in). 1995

Paradise Regained. Philip
Sajet. Automatic watches, gold.
Fabricated, assembled. 1995

Boxer Boys. Philip Sajet.
Silver, photographs. Fabricated,
assembled. Each
disk/photograph 5.5 cm (2¼ in).
1995

Christer Jonsson's imaginary miniatures are both objects and wearables and, in a way, consequent in their inconsistencies.

These strangely macabre, gazebo-like constructions combine a variety of forms, techniques and materials which include casting and fabrication, gilded and patinated silver, enamelling and anodized titanium. They are for the solitary gaze, evoking chance visitations in gardens of dreams and memories.

Jonsson's deliberately varietal approach lends conviction to the "garden" metaphor, but also to an impression of fragmentation and fantasy, order and disorder. This is emphasized at every turn. Parts revolve, or open and close. Generic simplification rubs shoulders with complex detail, the natural with the symbolic, disrupting a reading of scale, contributing to a state of disturbance, unease and unreality.

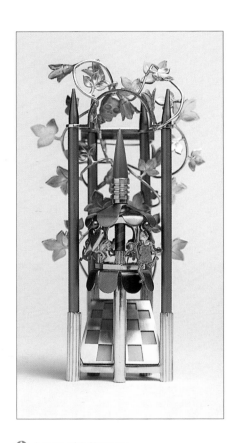

◆ **Garden with Merry-go-round. Christer Jonsson.**
Gilt, silver, titanium. Parts mounted by soldering, riveting and by screws, anodized, patinated. Merry-go-round can be turned.
13 x 6 cm (5⅛ x 2½ in). 1996

◆ **Black Virgin in Rose Garden. Christer Jonsson.**
Silver, gilt, enamel, brilliants. Parts mounted together by soldering, rivets and screws, enamelled, set stone. Doors can be open or closed. 13 x 5 cm (5⅛ x 2 in). 1997

◐ **Necklace:
Japanese Warrior
Samurai. Mary Ann
Scherr.** 14ct gold,
netsuke, sterling
silver, opal. Etched,
formed, fabricated,
riveted, oxidized.
36 x 6.5 cm
(14 x 2½ in). 1997

121

*Mary Ann Scherr is
best known in the
jewellery world for her
pioneering work on
the theme of body-
monitoring devices in
the late sixties and
early seventies. Her
other great interest
has been in the
process of abstract
ornamentation
through etching.*

*In this talismanic
pendant piece, Scherr
turns her attention to
a figurative theme,
setting a Japanese
warrior within a
classic gothic design
of chain and drops.*

THEMES & NARRATIVES

Eugenie Bell has immersed herself in the visual experience of Japan – not the Japan of motorcyles and pachinko parlours, but the Japan of craft reverence and serene temple gardens.

She has studiously and deliberately embraced the persuasive influence of this carefully maintained cultural milieu. Her conviction is that by analyzing and acting out its sensibilities and aesthetic determinants through her own work, as a non-Japanese, she will begin to forge an integrated lyric expression of and for East and West. The prize will be a language which is at once subtly cross cultural and authentically new.

⬡ **Scattered Light III. Eugenie Bell.** Sterling silver, 24 ct gold keum boo. Formed, fabricated, kuem boo gold application, 5 x 5 x 1 cm (2 x 2 x ⅜ in). 1996

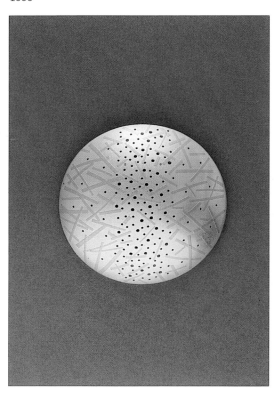

▶ Characteristic of the jewellery of Geoff Roberts is the large scale and the colourful metallic finish, achieved by heat printing acrylic, in blue, purple and red shades.

The use of acrylic, a lightweight material, enables him to create large scale pieces without, in a practical sense, the loss of wearability. His design process is intuitive, relying mainly on memory and a pair of shears, rather than preliminary sketches or specific research. Roberts develops his ideas during construction. After years of transforming acrylic into "supermetal", he now deliberately juxtaposes the latter with real metal which has been denuded of its natural metallic quality by galvanizing and oxidization.

His theatrical jewellery gives the impression of fantasy regalia, larger than human scale. Fish are a recurring motif. In many cultures they have symbolized fertility, abundance and averted all evil. The confident wearer might appear to be invested with such symbolic or ceremonial powers.

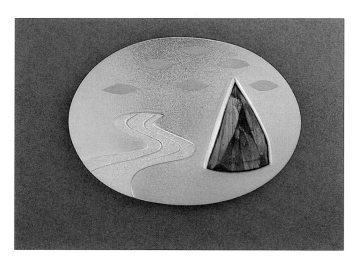

△ **Rock Garden (brooch). Eugenie Bell.** Sterling silver, fine gold, haematite crystal, Fabricated, rollerprinted, keum boo gold application. 3 x 6 cm (1¼ x 2¼ in). 1996

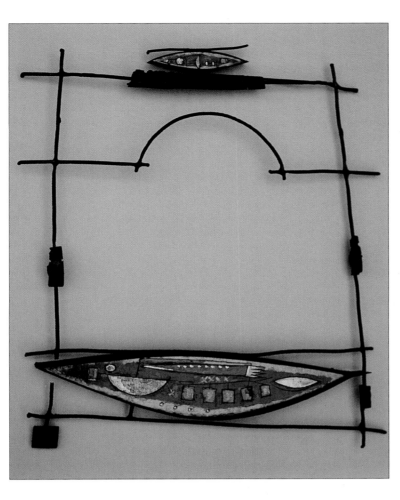

Floating Forms and Fifteen Kisses – Neckpiece. Geoff Roberts. Steel, leather, metal foils. Welded, printed. 49 x 44 x 3 cm (19¼ x 17¼ x 1¼ in). 1998

Boxed Tattoos. Geoff Roberts. Steel, leather, metal foils. Welded, printed. 41 x 39 x 5 cm (16¼ x 15¼ x 2 in). 1998

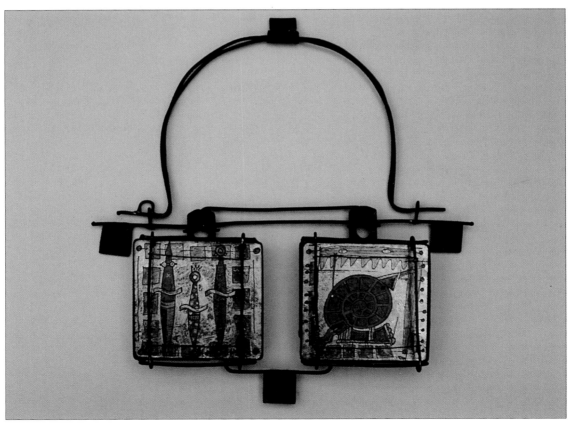

Pierre Cavalan's jewellery is exotic in its overall impression but comfortably familiar in its inner detail. His ironically architectonic and grandiose constructions resembling medals and other former expressions of social adhesion sit more or less within the postmodern genre of appropriation.

Cavalan evidently ridicules jewellery which is worn to signify membership of an institution or society. He parodies military decorations, insignia and ceremonial regalia, hinting that they have provided a sentimental glue but carry unconsidered meaning. Banal symbols, wartime souvenirs and magical tokens are all brought together, incorporating found or salvaged objects, which have no value in themselves but which benefit from the rich, jewel-like ornamentation that their accretion bestows. All these elements are woven into the web of ironic social and political commentary that is his signature.

Gun Control. Pierre Cavalan. Shells, bullet shell, biro case, costume jewellery, enamel badge, found objects. Soldered, riveted, set. 16 x 8.5 cm (6¼ x 3¼ in). 1996

Architectural forms, modelled into jewellery, are Vicki Ambery-Smith's trademark. Her interest in architecture is, as she herself states, untrained and purely visual. Virtual or fantasy monuments are reduced to miniature scale to be worn as brooches or earrings, or used as boxes. The historic association of jewellery with miniature worlds and indeed with architectural styles is thus realized.

The Romanesque and Renaissance periods, with the structural clarity and reduced ornament of their edifices, attract her attention in particular. It is therefore not surprising that Ambery-Smith is a fan of the architects Christopher Wren and Palladio, whose buildings are famous for their beauty and proportions. Her brooch "Temple of Jupiter" is a typical example, as it shows both a classical temple façade with columns and interior views of arches reminiscent of the Palladian villas of the Veneto. The temple is rendered in folded silver sheet with yellow gold details highlighting the structural elements, whilst the columns and carved and twisted wires form decorative details.

Ambery-Smith has evolved a very consistent and individual oeuvre.

⬭ **Temple of Jupiter.
Vicki Ambery-Smith.**
Sterling silver with yellow gold detail. Scored and folded sheet, twisted wire and carved chanier.
5 x 6 cm (2 x 2⅜ in). 1995

125

INDEX OF ARTISTS

The artists featured in this book are listed here in alphabetical order. The pages on which their work appears follow each entry. Their work is coded according to the following categories:

C: Commissions accepted
W: Workshops
V: Visits to the studio **by appointment only**

Christer Jonsson
Heleneborgsgatan 48 6tr
11732 Stockholm, Sweden
Tel/Fax: (08) 641 0564
ChristerJonsson@konstfack.se
C; W; V
page 120

Imke Jörns
Louisenstrasse 48 HH
01099 Dresden, Germany
Tel/Fax: (0351) 801 5066
V
pages 64–5

Vered Kaminski
23 Derech Beith-Lechem
93553 Jerusalem, Israel
Tel: (02) 671 5961
Fax: (02) 672 5807 (c/o M. F.)
C; W; V
pages 4, 19

Esther Knobel
39 Bezolel Street
Jerusalem 94556, Israel
Tel/Fax: (02) 2624 9978
C; W; V
page 29

Winfried Krüger
Seeberg 2
75175 Pforzheim, Germany
Tel: (07231) 68536
C; W; V
page 30

Claudia Langer
Steyrer Strasse 13
4470 Enns, Austria
Tel/Fax: (07223) 82592
e.langer@EUnet.at
C; W; V
page 115

Dongchun Lee
Sonkon-dong 339-32
Kyongju-shi, Kyongbuk, South Korea
page 48

Margrit Linder
Webereistrasse 33
8134 Adliswil, Switzerland
Tel: (01709) 1224
Fax: (01709) 1225
AdrianLinder@compuserve.com
C; W; V
page 99

Nel Linssen
Groesbeekseweg 197
6523 NS Nijmegen, The Netherlands
Tel/Fax: (024) 323 1765
http://www.homeworldonline.nl/~b.linssen.
C; V
pages 4, 42

Kadri Mälk
Sulevimägi 10-1
Tallinn 1, Estonia
Tel: (02) 641 1870
Fax: (02) 626 7350
C; W; V
pages 104–5

Amanda Mansell
45 Westbury Court
Nightingale Lane
London SW4 9AB, UK
Tel: (01582) 504452
C; W; V
pages 108–9

Bruce Metcalf
127 Birch Avenue
Bala Cynwyd
PA 19004, USA
(215) 763 6449
metcalf-lefoll@worldnet.att.net
W; V
pages 93, 96–7

Noon Mitchelhill
W6, Cockpit Workshops
Cockpit Yard
Northington Street
London WC1N 2NP, UK
Tel: (0171) 916 9013
Fax: (0171) 916 2455
C; V
page 59

Sonia Morel
Montagibert
1005 Lausanne, Switzerland
Tel: (021) 311 3250
Fax: (021) 312 0968
C; W; V
page 40

Ted Noten
Marnixkade 98 1
1015 ZJ Amsterdam, The Netherlands
Tel/Fax: (020) 638 0443
C; W; V
page 114

Tomasz Ogrodowski
Pracownia Plastyczna
Zgierska 75/81 m. 152 B
91465 Lódz, Poland
Tel/Fax: (042) 657 4448
page 61

Jacky Oliver
44B Muswell Hill
London N10 3JR, UK
Tel/Fax: (0181) 348 0350
C; V
page 91

Felicity Peters
20 Newbery Road
Wembley Downs
WA 6019, Australia
Tel: (08) 9341 8238
Fax: (08) 9245 8044
felicitypeters@hotmail.com
C; W; V
page 46

Annelies Planteydt
Marktplein 18
4421 JP Biezelinge, The Netherlands
pages 9, 36

Mah Rana
UK
Tel/Fax: (0171) 251 0110
http://www.brick.mcmail.com
C; W; V
page 112

Geoff Roberts
Louisville, 18 High Street
Portknockie
Buckie AB56 2LP, Scotland
Tel: (01542) 840 489
C; W; V
page 123

Jacqueline Ryan
Via San Prosdocimo, 19
35139 Padova, Italy
Tel/Fax: (049) 8724931
page 37

Philip Sajet
Muzenplein 2 (brughuis)
1077 WC Amsterdam, The Netherlands
Tel: (020) 679 8390
C; W; V
pages 118–9

Lucy Sarneel
Pesthuislaan 11
1054 RH Amsterdam, The Netherlands
Tel: (020) 616 5925
pages 16–7

Mary Ann Scherr
2132 Ridge Road
Raleigh
NC 27607, USA
Tel: (919) 783 7299
Fax: (919) 783 5992
mascherr@earthlink.net
C; W; V
page 121

Deganit Schocken
1 Yair Street
Baka
93503 Jerusalem, Israel
Tel: (02) 673 3359
Fax: (02) 654 1360
sharch@inter.net.il
C; W; V
pages 106–7

Theo Smeets
Fachhochschule Trier
Vollmersbachstr. 53a
55743 Idar-Oberstein, Germany
Tel: (06781) 946 314
renkel@fh-trier.de
C; W; V
pages 88–9

Etsuko Sonobe
Koufushi
Toukojichyo 1965-4
Yamanashi 400, Japan
Tel: (0552) 27 2237
Fax: (0552) 27 2247
C; V
page 43

Nicole Gratiot Stöber
for information contact:
Bernd and Irene Stöber
Wolfsbergallee 7
75177 Pforzheim, Germany
Tel: (07231) 582 117
pages 110–1

Rachelle Thiewes
5160 Cielo del Rio
El Paso
TX 79932, USA
Tel: (915) 833 0201
Fax: (915) 747 6749
W; V
pages 2, 74–5

Adele Tipler
@work
156 Brick Lane
London E1 6RU, UK
Tel/Fax: (0171) 377 0597
C; V
page 113

Silke Trekel
Unter dem Nussberg 8
06198 Kloschwitz ot Trebitz, Germany
Tel: (03451) 532 1959
Fax: (034607) 121 721
C; W; V
page 49

Manuel Vilhena
Strada Val Pallera, 23
10090 Gassino (To), Italy
Tel: (011) 960 5947
C; W; V
pages 22–3

Esther Ward
c/o Crafts Council
44a Pentonville Road
London N1 9BY, UK
Tel: (0171) 278 7700
Fax: (0171) 837 6891
C
page 44

Miranda Watkins
2.11 Oxo Tower Wharf
Bargehouse Street
London SE1 9PH, UK
Tel/Fax: (0171) 620 0330
C; V
pages 82–3

Kate Wilkinson
10 Haleacre Workshops
Watchet Lane
Little Kingshill
Bucks HP16 0DR, UK
Tel/Fax: (01494) 868332
C; V
page 76

Andrea Wippermann
Senffstrasse 9
06120 Halle, Germany
Tel/Fax: (0345) 550 5400
C; W; V
pages 26–7

Anette Wohlleber
Heidestrasse 35
73733 Esslingen, Germany
Tel: (0711) 32 2348 or (0711) 32 601 68
Fax: (0711) 32 804 93
design4eyes@compuserve.com
C; W; V
page 103

Mizuko Yamada
2-16-1 Ebisu-minami
Shibuya-ku
Tokyo 150-0022, Japan
Tel/Fax: (03) 3715 7534
mizuko@ibm.net
C; W; V
pages 32–3

Shiang-shin Yeh
6343 El Cajon Boulevard # 262
San Diego
CA 92115, USA
Tel/Fax: (213) 477 2211
syeh@ix.netcom.com/kevinyeh@usa.net
http://www.myart.com/yeh
C; W; V
pages 5, 47

Annamaria Zanella
Via Padana 99
S. Angelo di Piove
Padova 35020, Italy
Tel/Fax: (049) 584 1397
C; W; V
pages 20–1

Christoph Zellweger
8 Brincliffe Edge Road
Sheffield S11 9BW, UK
Tel/Fax: (0114) 255 4945
ccczell@dircon.co.uk
W; V
pages 34–5

GLOSSARY OF JEWELLERY TERMS

Anodizing *Development of a coloured surface layer which, depending on the parent metal, may involve the creation of a porous, surface oxide layer that may be dyed, or the passage of a controlled voltage over the parent metal within a chemical bath.*

Assemblage *Object made of (unrelated) things which are joined together, not necessarily by traditional goldsmithing techniques.*

Bezel *A thin, surrounding wall which is soldered, or otherwise attached to a piece and curved over a stone to retain it.*

Blackening *Creating a dark layer on the metal surface by oxidizing (see "oxidation").*

Die-cutting *Cutting shapes out of sheet material by passing through a profile made of a harder material.*

Electroforming *A form of electroplating in which a metallic surface is built up on a non-metallic substrate by the electrolytic deposition of metal atoms within a chemical bath.*

Enamelling *Decorative use of coloured glass by melting and fusing onto a surface or between wires.*

Etching *Erosion of a metal surface by corrosive agents, such as acids.*

Fabrication *Building a form by construction, from sheets or other parts, involving soldering or mechanical fixing.*

Fly-pressing *Mechanical process for forming sheet metal, using downward pressure provided by a spinning bar or "fly-wheel".*

Forging *Shaping metals, whilst hot or cold, using hammers, anvils or other metal surfaces.*

Fusing *Joining together metals by heating to melting temperature at the point or surface of contact.*

Gilding *Depositing of a fine layer of gold onto another metal using electrolysis (see "electroforming").*

Granulation *Fusing of small balls of metal onto a parent metal surface.*

Keum boo *A Korean technique in which a thin sheet of 24ct gold is fused to sterling silver, usually after a piece has been finished.*

Kiln-worked glass *Melting glass into moulds inside a kiln or oven.*

Lost wax casting *Reproduction of a form, originally wax, by pouring molten metal into a mould.*

Oxidation *Development of a naturally dark surface layer on metal alloys through the action of oxygen, by some combination of time, heat and chemicals.*

Photo-etching *Etching sheet metal by applying the intended surface pattern through a light-sensitized resist.*

Planishing *Systematic hammering technique, using polished tools, to smooth hand-raised surfaces.*

Repoussé *A decorative technique used to form metal, hammering from the back, using shaped punches.*

Slip cast porcelain *Creation of a hollow porcelain form by pouring liquid clay into a plaster mould which slowly absorbs moisture, leaving a dry outer shell of clay and a liquid inside which is poured out to create a hollow form.*

Spark erosion *Controlled method for cutting steel shapes involving the passage of an electric current through a copper tool, which "eats" away the steel at any point where the two metals are in contact.*

Spinning *Turning sheet metal into hollow forms by forcing over a wooden, metal or nylon shape called a chuck, while rotating it at high speed in a lathe.*

Tension systems *Reliance on stresses between fixed points for stability and form.*

Thermo-forming *Using heat in some way to soften a material, in order to change its shape.*

White-cooked silver *Chemical process, involving submersion of metal in hot acid solution, which causes the surface of silver to retain a matt white appearance.*

Wrought *General term referring to metals which are beaten into shape with tools (hand-wrought implies the use of hand tools only).*

Photography credits

Vicki Ambery-Smith 5t, 125; Satoshi Arai 39; Edward Barber 112tr; James Beards 31m/b; Jean Beining 9, 36; E. K. Bell 122; D Bers 88-89; Peter Bliek 4t, 42; Nina Broberg 120l; Sigurd Bronger 12-13; Monika Brugger 18; Stefania Capogna 124; Earl Carter 100b; Peter Chang 4b, 51; Lin Cheung 94; David Cripps 50; Joël Degen 6b, 41, 56, 58-59, 79, 112tl/b; Pierre Degen 98b; Helen Drutt Gallery, Philadelphia 106; Sean Ellis 109; Anne Finlay 57; Gerda Flöckinger 52; Jeremy Forster 84-85; Julia Forte 86r; Victor France 46; Karl Fritsch 87t/bl; André Geßner 27tr; David Gilliland 44; Natalie Gledhill 70-71; Kate Gollings 101; Karl Grant 77; Jochen Grün 62; Christoph Grunig 110-111; Tom Haartsen 67-69, 119t; Castello Hansen 7b; Minoru Hashimoto 10-11; Norman Hollands 54-55;

Gerlinde Huth 45; Mark Johnston 31t; Imke Jörns 64l; Stefan Källstigen 120r; Vered Kaminski 4m, 19; Sulev Keedus 105; Øysten Klakegg 81t; Klassekampen Newspaper 80br; Winfried Krüger 30; Otto Künzli 87br; Okinari Kurokawa 43; Vicky Lavender 78; Oded Lebel 107; David Liddle 72-73; Margrit Linder 99; John K Macgregor 6t, 90; Mauro Magliani 20; Jerzy Malinowski 61l/tr; Amanda Mansell 108; Hannah McPherson 76; Stepanka Meciarova 63; Sonia Morel 40; Sara Morris 28; Trish Morrisey 113; Andra Nelki 98t; Hitoshi Nishiyama 32bl/br, 33bl/br, 38; Jacky Oliver 91; Jan Otsen 118, 119b; Nicolai Perjesi 53t; Ramón Plà Isern 116-117; Maciej Plewinski 61br; Graham Pym 82, 83t; Geoff Roberts 123; Alfredo Rosado 102; Royal College of Art 22b, 95; Masatoshi Sasahara 32t, 33t; Isamu Sawa 7t, 100t; Scene Magazine 86l; Bernhard Schmid 103; Helga Schulze-Brinkop

26, 27l/br, 49, 60, 64-65; Nachum Slepak/Israel Museum, Jerusalem 29l; Franco Storti 21tl; Teigen 80t/bl, 81b; Rachelle Thiewes 2, 74-75; Frank Thurston 115; Lorenzo Trento 21tr/b, 74; Tetsuya Tsuji 24-25; Rob Turner 22t, 23; Diederik van der Donk 114; Tanel Veenre 104; Gregory Vinitsky/Leonid Kwitkowski Padrul - courtesy of Eretz Israel Museum 29r; Ole Voldbye 53b; Miranda Watkins 83b; Shiang-shin Yeh 5b, 47; Christoph Zellweger 34-35; Ron Zijlstra 16-17.

Dimensions

Where one measurement is given, the relevant dimension is indicated in the text. Two measurements are listed in the order height x width; three measurements are given as height x width x depth.

First published in 1999 by
New Holland Publishers (UK) Ltd
London · Cape Town · Sydney · Auckland

24 Nutford Place
London W1H 6DQ
United Kingdom

80 McKenzie Street
Cape Town 8001
South Africa

Unit 4, 14 Aquatic Drive
Frenchs Forest, NSW 2086
Australia

Unit 1A, 218 Lake Road
Northcote, Auckland
New Zealand

The right of David Watkins to be identified as the author of this work has been asserted by him in accordance with the Copyright, Design and Patents Act, 1988.

ISBN 1 85974 078 2

Editorial Assistant: Anke Ueberberg
Designer: Grahame Dudley
Project Editor: Rosemary Wilkinson

Editorial Direction: Yvonne McFarlane

Reproduction by Modern Age Repro House, Hong Kong
Printed and bound in Singapore by Tien Wah Press (Pte) Ltd

2 4 6 8 10 9 7 5 3

Dedication
I dedicate this book to young jewellers, from whom, in my time as a teacher, I have learnt and continue to learn so much about our art.

Author's Acknowledgements
I wish to thank Beatriz Chadour-Sampson, jewellery historian, for her generous assistance, and invaluable moral support, in the later stages of completing this book.

IMPORTANT
The copyright for the designs in this book is the property of the artists credited, unless otherwise stated. This book is intended purely as a source of inspiration. It is unlawful to exhibit copies of the designs in this book or use them for commercial gain or for anything other than personal or private purposes.